Happy at Homeschool

Your Custom Blueprint for Simplicity and Success

TŪGATE PRESS
AN IMPRINT OF REVELLO PRESS

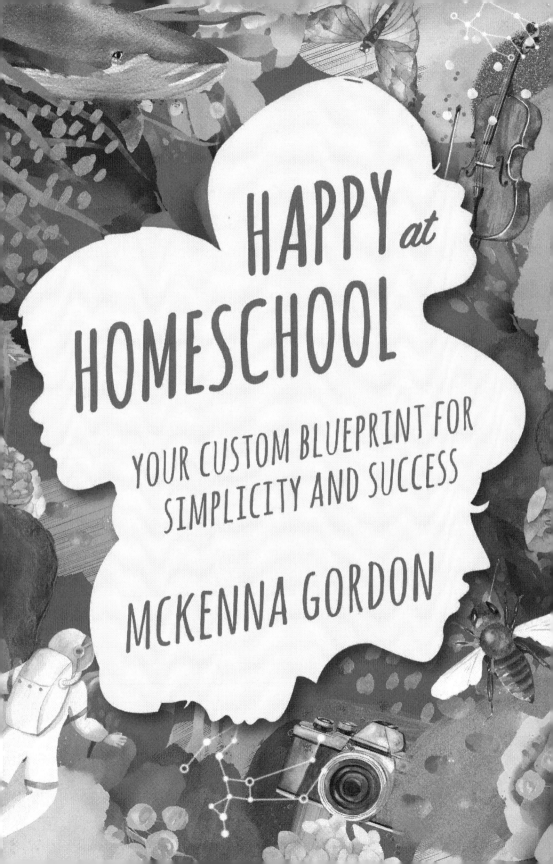

HAPPY AT HOMESCHOOL:
YOUR CUSTOM BLUEPRINT FOR SIMPLICITY AND SUCCESS

Tūgate Press
Imprint of Revello Press
P.O. Box 434
Pleasant Grove, UT 84062
www.revellopress.com

Copyright © 2020 McKenna Gordon
All rights reserved. Published 2020
Printed in the United States of America

ISBN-13: 978-1-931858-04-5
ISBN-10: 1-931858-04-7

All rights reserved under International and Pan-American Copyright Conventions. No part of this publication may be used, reproduced or transmitted in any form or by any means whatsoever, including but not limited to reproduction by electronic, mechanical or other means, including photocopying and recording, or by any information storage or retrieval system now known or to be invented, without express written permission from the publisher, except in the case of brief quotations used in reviews. Failure to comply with these terms may expose you to legal action and damanges for copyright infringement

The opinions and views expressed herein are the responsibility of the author and do not necessarily represent the position of the publisher.

Cover Design: McKenna Gordon
Interior Design: McKenna Gordon
Cover Design Floral Elements: Anna Babich
Cover Design Astronaut Illustration: Marina Ermakova
Cover Design Camera, Violin, and Whale Illustration: YesFoxy
Author Photograph: Rachel Gee

For more from McKenna Gordon, visit www.happyathomeschool.com

To Steve, Carter, Lorenzo, and Gabriella.
I love you with my whole heart.

Contents

I Would Never Homeschool 1

Your Personal Workshop 7

You Can Do This 17

Deschooling 25

Discovering Your Learning Philosophy 37
 Educational Philosophies, Approaches and Curricula 41
 Unschooling 44
 Waldorf 46
 Charlotte Mason Education 48
 A Thomas Jefferson Education (TJED) 50
 Classical Education 52
 Unit Studies 54
 Traditional (School at Home) 56

Curriculum 65

Tools for Planning Your Term, Unit, Month, or Week 81
 Cycling 81
 Course of Study 82
 Looping 83
 Block Scheduling 85
 Checklists 86
 Family Rhythm 87

Structuring Each Day 91
 Seven Hour School Days 92
 Compartmentalizing Knowledge Into Subjects 93

Teaching Multiple Ages   94
Putting It All Together   97

MOM CARE: HOW TO SURVIVE AND THRIVE 103

TEN HOMESCHOOLING MYTHS 123
Myth #1: "Homeschooled children aren't socialized."   124
Myth #2: "Homeschooling is expensive."   126
Myth #3: "I am not _____ enough to homeschool."
Myth #4: "My child might fall behind state standards."   130
Myth #5: "My children won't listen to me as their teacher."   131
Myth #6: "Homeschooled children are sheltered from the real world."   133
Myth #7: "My children will fight all the time if I homeschool."   135
Myth #8: "Homeschooled children miss out on important experiences."   136
Myth #9: "I will get sick of my children."   137
Myth #10: "High school subjects are difficult to teach at home."   138

YOUR CUSTOM BLUEPRINT 141

RECOMMENDED BOOKS, VIDEOS AND RESOURCES: 145

These are the differences between mind and heart as I now see them:
The mind is informed; the heart is inspired.
The mind feeds on facts; the heart feeds on truth.
The mind asks, 'Why?' The heart wonders, 'Why not?'
The mind is molded through questioning;
the heart asks its own questions.
The mind is verbose; the heart relishes brevity.
The mind seeks temporal and temporary pleasure;
the heart seeks spiritual and eternal joy.
The mind clings to reason; the heart clings to faith.
The mind often feels superior because of its vast knowledge;
the heart often feels humbled by all it doesn't yet understand.
The mind is critical; the heart is compassionate.
The mind thinks; the heart feels.
The mind seeks to be understood; the heart longs to understand.
The mind is knowledgeable; the heart is wise.

-Marlene Peterson

1. I Would Never Homeschool

I never imagined I'd homeschool my children. I was a full-time career builder and loved it. My oldest child attended day care, and as soon as he became old enough, I moved him to an academically rigorous private school. At age three, he spent 8 hours a day at this school while I was in the office. His brain and his personality seemed like the perfect match for this school, because he learns incredibly fast and he loves precision and perfection. The results of this private school's education philosophy in my child appeared to be very successful on the surface. He seemed to thrive there.

But a couple of years later, some things started changing in him. He started hating school and refusing to do work in the classroom. The school met with me numerous times to talk about this. They wanted him to skip a grade because they were having a hard time challenging him. But they were concerned with doing that, since their curriculum was already at least a year "ahead" of public school, and if I had any plans to pull him out of their expensive private school, it would make the problem even worse, because he would essentially be going "backwards" multiple grades if he ever transitioned to public school.

> "WE ASK CHILDREN TO DO FOR MOST OF A DAY WHAT FEW ADULTS ARE ABLE TO DO FOR EVEN AN HOUR. HOW MANY OF US, ATTENDING, SAY, A LECTURE THAT DOESN'T INTEREST US, CAN KEEP OUR MINDS FROM WANDERING? HARDLY ANY."
>
> JOHN HOLT

We had lots to think about during this time. And this was the first time I heard the call to homeschool. Looking back, I can see that I already knew it was where we'd end up, but I had fears about socialization and my ability to give him a complete education. I didn't allow myself to see it.

With my second child in preschool already, and knowing we wouldn't be able to afford the tuition of multiple children attending this school, we decided to pull my oldest from the private school and try public school. Public school counselors agreed he should skip a grade, but we wanted him with his peers. We opted for a Chinese immersion program–that would surely challenge his brain! And it did, for about a month. But it was just too slow for how his brain worked.

The next few months began a complete unraveling of my beliefs about school being an ideal place of learning for most children. As his brain worked so much faster than class was being taught, he stopped seeing the value of sitting in his chair in the classroom all day. He would tell me, "Mom, they're going over stuff I learned when I was three. I cannot just sit there, it's breaking my brain!"

He would tarry long in his bathroom breaks because he knew he wasn't missing anything he didn't already know. He had a hard time completing "busy-work" worksheets just for the sake of completing them. My son—who loves rules, who is not one to purposefully cause distractions, and who is not even very chatty—began losing every classroom privilege, including "bathroom privilege," (which I consider to be a right, not a privilege). He lost recess. He lost class parties. He even lost "Friday Fun" (an incentive where moms take turns bringing in a treat and an activity on Friday afternoons for all those who have been good little girls and boys) on the week that I was in charge of it. I played a game and did a craft with the rest of his class while he was sent to another classroom to catch up on his busy-work.

As a result of all this, the view he developed of himself is that he was the stupidest child in the class. Every single day, our car rides home included tears and, "I'm so, so stupid. I hate myself. I can't believe I didn't get to go to recess *again* today. What is wrong with me? Why can't I just make myself do their stupid worksheets so I can play with my friends?" Sometimes it would include, "I don't deserve to live."

He was six years old.

Before you assume that this was just a horrible school with horrible teachers, it was not. This was a highly-rated school and he had a team of two teachers whom I respect to this day. They seemed to truly care for him. They were working with us. They wanted to find creative ways to help him, but the system they had to work within simply couldn't adjust enough to accommodate his learning. I quickly began to see that school is a round hole and my child is a square peg. They don't go together.

My son's emotional state was alarming enough that we knew we needed to intervene swiftly. We decided we couldn't afford to wait until the end of the school year. We removed him from school during Christmas break and we started homeschooling *unprepared*.

We are now about to begin our eighth year of homeschooling. The reasons we *started* to homeschool were because we felt we had no choice and that it was the only option left for our child. What I didn't know at that time is that there really were a thousand other reasons we had yet to discover. Those are the thousand reasons we *continue* to homeschool. Not just our "square" peg children, but also the children whose learning styles and personalities would be a great fit for public school. I could write an entire book about these thousand reasons. It would include all the benefits of a custom education, all the concerns I have with a bureaucrat-designed school system, and all of the ways that it has been (believe it or not) *easier* on me as a parent compared to when my child was in public school. But if I distill it all down to one bottom-line reason we homeschool, it's because we absolutely *love* it.

Had I not had a "square peg" child, I don't know if we ever would have chosen homeschool. The thought of that makes me so sad, considering all the blessings we've experienced as a homeschooling family.

Whether you feel you're beginning your homeschool journey out of necessity or out of excitement to provide a custom education for your children, my hope is that you will get so much more than a plan out of this book. Invest some time in the journaling exercises at the end of each chapter. When you do, you will start to see your own beliefs and philosophies come to the surface. You'll discover that you have unique gifts and skills that qualify you to be an ideal teacher for your children. You'll discover so many resources, methods, and options that will allow you to create a wonderful learning environment in your home and your community. You can do this!

2. Your Personal Workshop

"How do I get started?" is such a loaded question when it comes to homeschooling. It's nothing like answering how to get started with a garden or how to change a tire on your car. Those things are fairly straightforward with much fewer variables than raising and educating the heart and mind of a child.

I would love to hand you the magic formula and to-do list which, as soon as everything is checked off, you will have reached the destination of being a very successful homeschooler. I would dictate to you the best curriculum for each subject and you could buy it and your children would get a deep and thoughtful education and become very happy humans. But one method that fits all? That's like saying every child has the same needs, interests, and learning style. That sounds like public school to me. One of the main draws to homeschooling is being able to provide a custom education for your child based on his/her specific *mission, gifts, needs, and interests*.

There are so many homeschooling guides and opinions out there. I feel a little annoyed when I see people explaining that they have found the perfect homeschooling "recipe" and are sharing it for everyone else to implement because it's a sure-fire, tried-and-true method. The truth is, no one can tell you how to homeschool. It's so personal, and most people are drawn to homeschooling *because* it is customizable.

I can't tell you how to homeschool, but I can help guide you in discovering the best method for your family. I love that homeschool isn't a conveyor belt where we all go along and end up at the same destination, finished and "ready for the world" precisely on schedule. Jump off the conveyor belt and explore! Be divergent! Take the scenic route, stop to smell the roses, spend time in the wild, grow at your own pace, follow what invigorates you, make deep anchoring connections with your children, and have fun!

Because you know your child better than anyone else, you can create a learning environment that cracks their heart wide open. And when a child's heart is wide open, their brain learns and retains information for life. More importantly, they develop a lifelong love for learning. So while I will share with you what has worked well for my family, this book is less about exactly how I homeschool and more about guiding you through creating your school into exactly what it needs to be for your family.

That's what this book is all about. Rather than all my opinions about home education, this book serves as your personal workshop, allowing you to discover and define what you value in education and then create a plan for your family. You probably have some deeply-held beliefs about learning, family culture, and personal progression that have never been brought to your consciousness.

PLEASE take the time to follow the journal prompts in this book. When you do, you will have many brilliant and wonderful ideas flow into your mind that are inspired just for your family. When you're finished, you will have a complete blueprint for starting your homeschool journey in confidence. Not confidence in my plan, your neighbor's plan, or Sally the Super Homeschool Overachiever Mom's plan, but a plan designed by the only two people who have the insight, intuition, and authority to do so: your child's parents.

Does this mean you'll be set for life with your blueprint and things will always be easy and successful? Absolutely not. But it's the best way to get a solid starting point. Your blueprint will grow and evolve over time to meet the ever-changing needs of your growing children. But that is one of the beauties of homeschool. It can revolve around your family unit rather than your family unit revolving around school. Doesn't that seem like how it should be?

Let's talk about educating the heart before the mind. Do you have seemingly random yet vivid memories of how you learned certain things in life? For some reason, I have a vivid memory of how I learned the definition of the word *siphon*. My dad and I were moving a water bed (remember those?) from one bedroom to another. The waterbed was going to be mine and I was so excited.

We needed to empty the waterbed to move it, so he used a garden hose going from the waterbed out the second floor window of our house to create a siphon. I remember him explaining to me how a siphon worked. I thought it was such a funny word. As an adult, whenever I hear the word siphon, I flash back to that time with my dad. Every single time! It's an anchoring memory that happened to have education attached to it.

Of course, I could have learned the word siphon by reading the dictionary or having it assigned as a vocabulary word in school. Eventually I would have remembered that word long-term. But that day, my dad educated my heart. I was spending quality time with my father, while getting a real-world example of how a siphon works. And I was emotionally invested, because this was going to be my waterbed after it was moved to my room. My heart was in it first—and that opened the channel for my mind to grasp and retain very detailed information about how a siphon works, at a very young age!

> "WE SHALL NOT CEASE FROM EXPLORATION AND THE END OF ALL OUR EXPLORING WILL BE TO ARRIVE WHERE WE STARTED AND KNOW THE PLACE FOR THE FIRST TIME"
>
> -T.S. ELIOT

It's not to say that memorizing facts with a closed heart doesn't ever work. I graduated from high school with great grades even though my heart was only sometimes open to what was being taught. But mostly, I was not emotionally invested in what I was learning. It was just assigned to me. I didn't get to decide what to learn. As one of the brightest kids in my school, I still thought that the reason for all of this learning was just a means to an end: pass the test, get the grade, get the diploma, done. Education as a destination. As a result of my brain being the only thing that was taught, without my heart being taught first, I remember very little of what I learned in high school history and science.

As we slowly discovered that homeschool was what was right for our family, I started developing a very strong personal philosophy on education. That philosophy has strengthened over time as I've put it into practice and watched my children open their hearts to learning. On this journey, I have had the wonderful opportunity of learning so much more than I learned in high school, because by educating my childrens' hearts, I've also re-educated my own.

The T.S. Eliot quote above embodies how I learn as an adult, and I remember learning this way as a very young child. But there was also this long period of time where I thought that the only things that could be learned through wonder and adventure and magical exploration were music and art. Those things have always been magical to me.

But why not math? Why not science? Why not history? At some point in many students' lives, those subjects become more about memorizing facts, surviving the semester, and doing just enough to get a solid B on their report card so they can finally close the textbook for good. End the chore. Check the box.

I wonder… was Einstein's journey to discover the energy equivalence formula a chore? Was da Vinci's time investment in exploring architecture and engineering an annoyance? Did Nikola Tesla essentially usher in the age of electrical power to check a box? Or is it that math, science, engineering, and architecture were their magical subjects, just like music and art are mine?

Is it possible for every subject to be explored unceasingly, passionately, and with a spirit of adventure and wonder? Would we learn more?

As you read through this guide, I will invite you to ponder and journal some questions that will help you develop your own education philosophy, and eventually an entire plan for your homeschool year.

Your answers to these questions will evolve over time. But you've got to start somewhere. If you don't have an opinion about these things, you'll be like a dry leaf in the wind, floating purposeless in whichever direction you're blown, crumbling easily under stress.

Please take at least five minutes to journal each question. Don't "binge read" this book and skip the journaling. Each step in this workbook will build upon the previous. Your answers to these questions will anchor your heart on the tough days. The days you wonder if you're doing enough and if the plan you created for your family is "working." The days you feel tempted to compare your child's education to someone else's. Prayerfully come back to these questions often and come up with more questions of your own to answer.

My Beliefs About Education

What is education? What is knowledge? What is wisdom? How do these things differ?

_____
_____
_____
_____
_____
_____

What does it mean to be properly educated? What are the fruits of having had a proper education?

_____
_____
_____
_____
_____
_____

*What does it mean to be
successful in life?*

_____

_____

_____

_____

_____

What does it mean to be properly socialized?

_____

_____

_____

_____

_____

*Does public school do a statistically good job of
turning out properly educated, successful, and socialized children? If so, how does it do a good job? If
it fails, how does it fail?*

_____

_____

_____

_____

_____

What are the learning styles of each of my children? (Auditory, visual, kinesthetic.)

What is my learning style?

3. You Can Do This

My personal learning philosophy is long and evolving, but the roots of it have never changed. Here are my roots:

> We as parents have been given the divine stewardship to raise our children in love, safety, and righteousness. I believe that parents are a child's best teachers and that the home (more specifically alongside family, regardless of location) is the ideal setting for learning and becoming. Play is the work of childhood. When children's hearts are educated first, through beautiful art, inspiring music and books, and an atmosphere of safety and play, they will naturally enter a love of learning phase that is so exciting to witness! As we allow our children to lead their education through their own interests and inspiration, we facilitate a lifelong passion for learning and growth.

Society has done a great job of convincing us that professionals are best suited to take care of, raise, and teach children. This is not true. My friend Becky Pitcher, editor of *Seek Learning* magazine once said, "If God wanted schools and doctors to raise children, then he would not have given us the structure of the family. It is your divine privilege and stewardship to rear your children in love and righteousness."

In the book, *Hold On To Your Kids*, Gabor Mate says, "The modern obsession with parenting as a set of skills to be followed along lines recommended by experts is, really, the result of lost intuitions and of a lost relationship with children... Parenthood is being undermined."

I constantly have people share with me that they feel they should homeschool their children, but they know they can't because (fill in the blank). I wish so badly that I could help all good parents believe this:

> "DON'T QUESTION YOUR ABILITY TO TEACH YOUR CHILD. QUESTION PUTTING YOUR CHILD INTO THE SAME SYSTEM THAT LEFT YOU FEELING INCAPABLE OF TEACHING YOUR CHILD."
>
> -UNKNOWN

YOU were called to be your child's parent. YOU are endowed with knowledge and inspiration on what their heart needs. If what they need right now is to not participate in the public school system and instead to gather as a family to learn and grow together, then that righteous desire will be placed in your heart. Please trust that desire. Please trust that prompting and know that God has entrusted YOU as well. Ask Him to release fear from your heart. Ask Him to clear your mind of worry over judgment from friends or family, and from fear of your own inadequacies. Ask Him to show you how you are already so very qualified to be the one to teach your children the most important things they need in this life, both spiritual and secular.

> "THE CALLING TO BE A PARENT INCLUDES THE GIFT TO TEACH IN WAYS THAT ARE RIGHT FOR YOU AND YOUR CHILDREN."
>
> ROBERT D. HALES

Trust yourself the way He trusts you. Trust that you do know your child, and if you don't yet know them well, trust that you have the ability, authority, and gift to know deeply who they are. Who is your child? Why are they here? What are their gifts? What makes them special? What makes them divergent? And is the way they are being educated supporting them in these things?

I could list so many reasons why I am unfit to homeschool my children or even be a mother. I am easily overwhelmed. I mess up every single day. I've got a temper and sometimes act like a martyr. Though I am naturally the life of the party with friends, I often feel like I'm way too serious as a mom and forget to have fun with my kids (to the point that one of my kids sometimes jokingly refers to me as, "The Fun Sucker," because I suck the fun out of his life).

I sometimes let myself feel really bad about all of this, but you know what else is true? I am *serious* about being a mother. I make child psychology a personal hobby. I research my children's health problems like an FBI agent. I create and teach group classes just so my kids can be students in them. I cook healthy-ish food from scratch daily because of special dietary needs. I'm constantly tweaking our schedule and our systems to keep our home a safe and peaceful place where passionate learning and rich tradition can flourish. I'm a warrior for my children and they have no doubt that they are loved and supported. I always apologize. I'm a safe parent. And that's perfect because it's what they need. They need *me*. They need who I am. They need a mom with my flaws and they need to witness me work through them, tirelessly trying again and again to improve myself. Of all the things I am not, I remind myself today that I am every single thing they need in a mom.

What kind of mom or dad are you? Do you realize that you are enough for them? Focus on magnifying your strengths, for they outweigh your weaknesses, and God will make your weak things become strong unto you.

You do not need to be a perfect parent with perfect children in order to be successful at homeschooling. Unless you are physically or emotionally damaging your children, you don't even need to be a *better* parent than you currently are. I promise that if you ponder deeply and seek God's guidance, your weaknesses can become strengths through your homeschooling journey.

I Can Do This

Who is my child? Why are they here and what gifts have they been given? What makes them special and divergent?

_____
_____
_____
_____
_____
_____

Is my child's education currently supporting them in these things? How? How not?

_____
_____
_____
_____
_____
_____

As a parent, I have been given special gifts and abilities that help me be the parent my children need. My gifts are...

_____
_____
_____
_____
_____
_____

My gifts and abilities allow me to teach, guide, and mentor my children in these ways

_____
_____
_____
_____
_____
_____
_____

Our family school will be strong in these areas:

_____
_____
_____
_____
_____
_____
_____
_____
_____

4. Deschooling. Do You Really Need to Do It?

You may or may not have heard of deschooling. If you have, I already know you want to skip this chapter. I always want to skip it, too. TOO BAD. YOU NEED TO DO THIS.

If you ever attended school or if your children ever attended school, even if they've only attended kindergarten, your brain is ingrained with how school *should be*, but that is merely based on how school *is*. But just because something *is* a certain way, is that the way it *should* be? It's really difficult for the human mind to break away from what *is* or what "always has been" (according to our own experience) and to fully accept a new way of doing things.

It's every new homeschooler's human nature to tend toward re-creating public school at home. But the fact of the matter is, recreating school at home just doesn't work. School is designed to accommodate large numbers of students at once. It's at least as much about classroom management and crowd logistics as it is about curriculum. So to recreate the schedule, structure, rules, and learning environment at home not only conflicts with how a home works, it also causes you to miss out on learning opportunities. You can fight this tendency to re-create school at home all you want, but that programming will remain in your brain and your child's brain until you both take a period to "detox," or "deschool."

> "I SUPPOSE IT IS BECAUSE NEARLY ALL CHILDREN GO TO SCHOOL NOWADAYS AND HAVE THINGS ARRANGED FOR THEM THAT THEY SEEM SO FORLORNLY UNABLE TO PRODUCE THEIR OWN IDEAS."
>
> AGATHA CHRISTIE

For fun, let's say that public school bandwidth is 50% curricula and 50% logistics (it's much less favorable than this, but just for illustration sake, we'll go with 50/50.) What if you could take away the burden of classroom management and the logistics of dealing with issues such as school policy, changing classrooms, lining up, and more? That frees up so much bandwidth that can be used for effective learning.

Homes are dynamic places filled with people of many different ages. There are places for gathering and places for being alone. During a normal school's learning time, there are also meals being prepared and laundry being cycled. Interruptions from toddlers and Amazon deliveries, phones ringing, and more. Trying to layer a public school schedule and method over the everyday workings and schedule of managing a home is daunting. *(It's why I felt so much sympathy for those who were forced into "homeschool" because of the school closures around Covid-19. I couldn't imagine what these wonderful mothers and fathers were trying to attempt! Recreating public school at home with everything else going on had to be overwhelming. I imagined it would turn everyone off to the idea of homeschooling because of how difficult it might have been. If you are one of those parents, my hat's off to you!)*

Rather than recreate what's happening at school, you're better off creating a method that works with the flow of your home and family. Because attempting this is so difficult, and because it is everyone's instinct is to recreate school at home rather than create something new and better, it is so important to take your brain through a "detox" period. Without deschooling for a period of time, you are much more likely to experience friction with your children, enforce schedules and teach curriculum that are disliked by all (including you), feel inadequate, and eventually throw in the towel.

You don't need to try to be a public school teacher in your house. Your children don't need to sit at desks or raise their hand to comment. You don't need to ring the starting bell at 8:45 a.m. or spend at least 30 minutes on math each and every day. You don't need to follow common core. Get all of this out of your head for the time being.

How long do you need to deschool? A common opinion is to deschool one month for every year your child spent in public school. I think in some cases it can be done faster, and in others it takes much more time. Factors include personality and how strong your inclination is to re-create school at home. Don't count summer vacation time as as deschooling time.

So what does deschooling look like? Does learning even occur? Will your children lose information and go backwards a grade? Let me paint the picture for you.

Deschooling looks like reading books, visiting libraries and museums, trying out co-ops, planning meals, making grocery lists, bargain shopping and cooking food together, exploring nature, hiking, making art, having dance parties, learning to crochet, learning to sew, learning to build a fire, learning to change a tire, building a huge fort and having a read-a-thon, watching documentaries, traveling, doing family history work, journaling, learning a new musical instrument, assisting parents with things like home repairs, building projects, car maintenance, mowing the lawn, serving neighbors, putting on puppet shows and backyard plays, mastering the cartwheel, learning photography, creating a story and writing it down.

Do not complete a single worksheet. Do not take one single quiz. Do not give one writing assignment.

You will begin to see your children transform. Their creativity will come alive. They'll complain of being bored less and less as their minds will be active and inventive more and more. You'll begin to see that learning happens all the time. You will start to realize that you cannot stop your children from learning. Only when you see this, with your very own eyes, in your very own children, can you stop stressing out about whether you are "doing enough."

If people ask you, "How many hours a day do you do school?" You can say, "Twelve." Or, in the words of Becky Pitcher, you can say, "We are deschooling so that my children learn how to follow their interests, so that I stop associating learning with the classroom and my kids stop associating learning with discomfort."

Stop associating learning with discomfort!

We are on this earth to learn and to progress. Yet we are that we might have JOY! Those two statements should not be incongruent! That joy is meant to *come from* our learning, progression, and creation. What a clever counterfeit of truth it is to turn learning and progression into a forced and boring task, torturous at worst and to be tolerated at best.

> "WHEN THE ATMOSPHERE ENCOURAGES LEARNING, THE LEARNING IS INEVITABLE."
>
> ELIZABETH FOSS

During this deschooling process, you will discover more of your child's passions, and probably more of your own! If you don't already know it, you will discover how your child learns best: through reading or listening, through hands-on work, through outside discovery, through relationships, or through other ways. Be observant, as this will help you choose curricula that is best suited for your child. You will have time to make meaningful connections with your children and recalibrate your family. This is a time of rest, exploration, growth, and gathering.

Deschooling is the hardest thing to do. The *way* of it is easy. The mind games you will play with yourself are the difficult part.

Remember, you've been trained to feel like you aren't fit to teach your children. You may feel yourself begin to develop a chip on your shoulder or that you need to prove to your neighbors or to nosy Aunt Gertrude that your child is learning at the same pace as when he was in public school. You will be tempted to look for proof of learning in the form of checked-off boxes, worksheets, quizzes, and penmanship. IGNORE these thoughts and inclinations. There is a time for these things, if they fit in to your child's learning style, but it is not during deschooling.

The other beautiful thing that deschooling provides is the ability to start unprepared. Remember shortly before you became a parent, how you kept telling yourself you're not quite ready? You needed to learn this first, or get that thing in place first, or finish painting the kitchen first, or read all the parenting books? And then the baby is on the way and you wonder if you did all the things to prepare yourself or if you're going to fail miserably...and now the baby is here and suddenly you are blindsided with more love than you knew you were even capable of. You were imbued with more intuition and strength than you thought you had in you. Suddenly all the parenting books flew out the window and you stepped up to the plate. You *became a real parent*. And you realized that it didn't matter if you had the kitchen painted before the baby came because she's here now and your entire world is different.

You're never going to be "ready" to homeschool. Start unprepared. Deschool for several months and give yourself time to adjust to having your children with you all the time. Give yourself the time to figure it out *while* you're in the thick of it. Detox your brain from the need to check boxes and finish math by 10:40 because at 10:45 is when history class begins.

If you don't deschool, there will come a time when you realize homeschooling is not working. It's not fun for your children, it's not fun for you, and you're at your wits end. You will then either quit and send your children back to school or you will "take a break" for several months, but either way, you'll feel like a homeschool failure. If you end up taking a break, that will essentially be deschooling, but it won't be as effective if it isn't done intentionally. So save yourself that mental breakdown and just "take the break" now. It's called deschooling.

How do you know your deschooling is "complete"? You will notice your child's behavior shift. Rather than feeling bored frequently, they'll learn to fill that boredom with learning (which doesn't feel to them like learning). You'll see them come up with projects, games, and inventions. They might navigate to the piano to make up a song. They might write a story just because an idea popped into their head. They'll make backyard messes which to them aren't messes at all, but kingdoms of wonder and delight. They will ask you to help them find tutorials and documentaries on things that pique their interest.

As your children do these things, you'll begin to notice that jumping on a trampoline and swinging on swings is teaching them physics. Playing with legos is teaching them problem solving, coding logic, and even math. Baking brownies is strengthening their executive function, math skills, and teaching science. Reading great literature is not just increasing their reading skills, but teaching values, ethics, creative thinking, history, and more.

And if all your child wants to do for two weeks is practice beat-boxing? Guess what? It's proven to strengthen vocal cords, increase breath control, improve creativity, and activate areas of the brain used for speech and reading. If beat-boxing can do that, imagine what starting a worm farm in a bucket in the backyard or learning to fly a drone and shoot and edit drone videos are teaching them! (All of these are personal examples.) Let your child be the guide during deschooling (and forever).

Take the time to journal the following questions. You may find that you have some fears to work through. They are valid hesitations, but journaling them can help you find the root of the fear, and eventually a solution.

My Deschooling Plan

What hesitations or fears do you have around taking a period of time to deschool?

_____
_____
_____
_____
_____
_____
_____
_____
_____

*What belief or knowledge do you hold
that creates this hesitation?*

_____
_____
_____
_____
_____
_____

*Imagine a future in which you deschooled and it
was incredibly successful. What does that look like
for each of your children? How could their hearts
and minds change?*

_____
_____
_____
_____
_____
_____
_____
_____
_____
_____
_____
_____

Brainstorm ideas about how you want your deschooling period to look.

5. Discovering Your Learning Philosophy

During your period of deschooling, I suggest reading about the different learning philosophies to discover what resonates most powerfully with you. There may be one philosophy that sings the song of your heart precisely. Or, you may find that several philosophies have elements that feel right for you and your family, and you can adopt the parts that work for you and leave the rest. I'm a very eclectic homeschooler. I can't say that I align 100% with any one philosophy. Rather, our way of doing things is a living, breathing philosophy that is slightly different for each child. It also evolves over time as my children grow and their needs change.

Here's an example of how our approach has evolved as my children have grown. When my children were younger, we did a lot of what people call "Unit Study." It's where you choose a subject of study and look at it from many different angles. I took it a step further and rather than choosing the subject for my children, I would watch and listen for things they were interested in.

My oldest was in first grade when we began homeschooling. At the time, he was so enthralled by snakes that it became our unit study. Snakes were part of all of his subjects. Reading, writing, science, history, art, math–all snakes. Yes, snakes were our math! You can add and subtract snakes, and I suppose you can even divide snakes (ew).

As soon as his interest for snakes began to wane, we moved on to his newest love: turtles. And so on. Through the eyes of my son, we were just exploring something he loved. But he was also getting a well-rounded education in the meantime. Through this experi-

> "EDUCATION DOESN'T NEED TO BE REFORMED. IT NEEDS TO BE TRANSFORMED. THE KEY TO THIS TRANSFORMATION IS NOT TO STANDARDIZE EDUCATION, BUT TO PERSONALIZE IT, TO BUILD ACHIEVEMENT ON DISCOVERING THE INDIVIDUAL TALENTS OF EACH CHILD, TO PUT STUDENTS IN AN ENVIRONMENT WHERE THEY WANT TO LEARN AND WHERE THEY CAN NATURALLY DISCOVER THEIR TRUE PASSIONS."
>
> SIR KEN ROBINSON, "THE ELEMENT"

ence, I solidified a major, unchanging portion of my personal education philosophy: *passion-based learning is the most powerful type of learning. When we are excited about the topic we're studying, learning is fast, deep, and long-term.*

As my son grew older, this method of learning grew up with him. We evolved into what I call "learning rabbit holes." One of my favorite examples of a learning rabbit hole is when my oldest was in about third grade. We chose *The Lion, the Witch and the Wardrobe* as our family read-aloud. Until I read it aloud to my children, I had forgotten that the premise of the story, the entire reason the characters went to live with Professor Digory (whose home contained the magical wardrobe leading to Narnia), is because it was set in World War II. All children were evacuated from London to live in the countryside where it was safer. I took no thought of this when I read this book as a child, but my children were curious about why the characters in the story had to leave their parents.

This led us on a two-week journey of learning about World War II. During that time, my kindergartner and third grader learned (and retain to this day) more information than I remember learning about that war during high school.

We learned what it would have been like to be a child during WWII. We looked at ration books. (I didn't even know what these were before going on this learning journey *with* my children!) We learned about and planted our own victory garden. (Did you know that the United States would not have been successful in WWII if it weren't for Americans planting victory gardens? We had enough food to either feed our soldiers or feed our citizens. Not both. Everyone did their part and planted gardens as big as they could to feed their own families so that all national reserves could feed the soldiers. I didn't know this heart-warming fact and we discovered layers of important lessons in just this one aspect of WWII.)

We found online recordings of then-Princess Elizabeth, who was a young teenager at the time. She and Princess Margaret broadcasted a regular radio show for the children of England to boost morale during the war. What a treasure that these things were recorded so that we could get a glimpse of the war through the eyes of children.

To this day, my children can spout off just as many–or more—facts about World War II than most college graduates I know. But the value is less in the facts and more in the heart-felt lessons they learned through this "unit study." And all of it started in Chapter Two of a well-loved classic. All of it started because they were invested in and concerned for the characters in this book. Their hearts were open. The fact that I had a gap in my own education with regard to WWII didn't affect my ability to be the most powerful ~~teacher~~ *facilitator* of my children's learning.

Now that my oldest is a teenager, his learning has evolved even more. I now "outsource" his math to a group tutor because I only advanced through Algebra 2 in my own schooling, and it's not something I wanted to learn in order to teach him. He is likely to be the calculus and statistics type of guy, so I became his facilitator and connector. (Sometimes being the best mentor for your child means finding someone else to be the best mentor for your child.) His focus now is first: developing life skills, emotional skills (E.Q.), and relationships. Second: preparing to get the best score possible on the ACT, as most colleges throughout the country love it when homeschoolers with decent ACT scores apply. No diploma needed. Many colleges have noticed that homeschoolers think outside the box and succeed in their programs, which makes them look good. Colleges want to look good. Colleges love homeschoolers. But that is another book to write.

Hopefully this illustrates how your learning philosophy becomes your core, but the approach you take can change year by year, and evolve and "grow up" with your children.

Educational Philosophies, Approaches and Curricula

Before you even think about purchasing curriculum, you need to discover your education philosophy. What do you believe about learning? Hopefully your journaling experience in the Your Personal Workshop chapter was enlightening. It's also helpful to talk to other homeschoolers and read up on different approaches. But I don't recommend worrying about curricula until you have a firm grasp on what your own learning beliefs are. If you do, there's a high chance you'll buy a curriculum that you end up disagreeing with or not enjoying.

Many people focus on curriculum when they first start to homeschool because they believe that learning happens best at school. Their approach is to try to simply measure up to school by using a curriculum that replicates what happens there. Others opt for whatever curriculum promises to be the easiest to teach or ones that are popular and recommended by others. Phrases like "open-and-go" or "done-for-you" are popular curricula features. While there's nothing at all wrong with these, I'm recommending that you pause first to make sure that curricula you use has the content and approach that aligns with what your family needs. You don't want to end up wasting money and becoming frustrated with something that's a bad fit.

Next you'll find the most common homeschool philosophies and methods. I'll give a short description of each and provide some books and resources so you can learn more. Please don't feel overwhelmed. Remember, this is a journey. Remember you have deschooling time to figure this out. Remember that this can evolve to cater to your children's learning styles, maturity, family needs, and life seasons.

This simple list of approaches to homeschooling represents all of the major homeschooling philosophies. You could also invent your own, but these are wonderful starting points. As you read through these ideas, some of them will be easy to eliminate. Some will make your heart sing. Several will probably feel acceptable to you. Dive deeper into those you feel would be a good fit for your family by reading the books or watching the videos I list next to each one.

As you explore, write down ideas you love from each approach–they're all full of wonderful ideas, and some of them will speak to you!

Unschooling

Main Tenet:

Children learn best through living life.

Approach:

Kids learn math through budgeting or starting a small business. They learn fractions through cooking. They learn to read by reading (anything they want, even if it's comic books). They learn physics by jumping on a trampoline and tumbling. No assignments and no formal curricula. Learn to code, cook, restore cars, sew, make movies, or trade stock: your child learns what they want, when they want.

Curricula:

No formal curricula.

Learn More:

Passion-Driven Education: How to Use Your Child's Interests to Ignite a Lifelong Love of Learning, Connor Boyak

WellEducatedHeart.com: This is a hybrid of unschooling and Charlotte Mason (children are free to learn what they're interested in, but they do so through rich literature, nature, and art.) Click on Mother's University. I highly recommend Mother's University class (it's free) for all, even if you don't feel drawn to unschooling. A great thing to listen to in little bits each day while you're deschooling.

Waldorf

Main Tenet:

Nature, creative expression, cooperation, play-based learning, social responsibility.

Approach:

Waldorf Education was developed by Rudolf Steiner in the early 1900s. It involves three stages of development. The first stage is from birth through age 7. During that stage there is no direct teaching and an emphasis on creative play and experiencing the world. From age 7 through age 14, lessons are approached through art. From age 14 to the end of high school, the approach is rigorous academics with a focus on learning to think for oneself.

Curricula:

WaldorfEssentials.com

EarthSchooling.info

Learn More:

Understanding Waldorf Education: Teaching from the Inside Out, Jack Petrash

WaldorfInspiredLearning.com

Charlotte Mason Education

Main Tenet:

Children are people in the image of God, not clay to be molded.

Approach:

Based on the teachings of educator Charlotte Mason. Let children delve deeply into beautiful art, nature, literature, poetry, and math so they will learn to recognize what is beautiful and wholesome in life.

Curricula:

CharlotteMasonHomeschooling.com

Amblesideonline.org (free study outlines)

Learn More:

For the Children's Sake: Foundations of Education for Home and School, Susan Schaeffer Macaulay

Simplewonders.org combines a Charlotte Mason approach with teachings of The Church of Jesus Christ of Latter-day Saints.

A Thomas Jefferson Education (TJED)

Main Tenet:

Gain a leadership education by studying the same way heroes throughout history learned.

Approach:

Historic heroes learned by wrestling with big ideas and reading great literature and deep philosophy. This is replicated under the direction of powerful mentoring (by the parent, and possibly other mentors). Raise children who can think independently, debate, work, and accomplish goals. There are three main educational phases that humans naturally go through: Core phase somewhat resembles unschooling in the younger years. Children naturally progress into "Love of Learning" phase where they dabble in lots of different interests. Around age 12-16, children naturally enter the Scholar phase, where they hone in on one or two main areas of interest and become deep scholars in that subject.

Curricula: L.E.M.I. Projects (Leadership Education Mentoring Institute)

Learn More:

A Thomas Jefferson Education: Teaching a Generation of Leaders for the Twenty-First Century, Oliver DeMille

TJED.org
TJED-mothers.org

Classical Education

Main Tenet:
Children learn in 3 stages: Grammar, Logic, and Rhetoric.

Approach:
During the Grammar stage there is lots of memorization of poems, songs, and stories. Logic phase teaches them to think about things they've learned and connect ideas to their life. Rhetoric phase teaches youth to express their ideas through writing, speech and debate.

Curricula:
Classical Conversations

Memoria Press

Story of the World

The Ordinary Parent's Guide to Teaching Reading

Learn More:
The Well-Trained Mind: A Guide to Classical Education at Home, Susan Wise Bauer

WellTrainedMind.com

Unit Studies

Main Tenet:

Rather than separating learning into subjects like reading, science, math, etc., find connections in everything.

Approach:

Choose a topic of interest and dive in! Study together as a family. When you read *Little House on the Prairie*, you're studying language arts, but you can also incorporate history, geography, art, cooking, science, and even math. You can cook pioneer meals over a fire, churn butter, sew your own doll, memorize famous poetry about early America, be inspired by art and sing songs from the time period, or anything else that sounds fun and interesting. You can make a unit study on anything. A classic book, a time period or an event in history, flowers, a country or a state, lizards, a movie, a Bible story, a Shakespeare play… you get the idea.

Curricula:

Moving Beyond the Page

Gather Round Homeschool

UnitStudy.com

The Good and the Beautiful (science programs are Unit Study based)

Pinterest (seriously, choose something you're interested in and type "Botany Unit Study," "Scotland Unit Study," "Walt Disney Unit Study," "Marine Biology Unit Study," "Narnia Unit Study.")

Learn More:

The Brave Learner: Finding Everyday Magic in Homeschool, Learning, and Life, Julie Bogart

Teaching From Rest, Sarah Mackenzie

Traditional (School at Home)

Main Tenet:

Public school at home.

Approach:

Parallels a typical classroom. Grade-level textbooks, workbooks, and teacher's manuals are used. Parents act as formal teachers. Tests, grades, and schedules are a normal part of traditional schooling. Families using this approach will have a mini-classroom set up in their home.

Curricula:

Abeka

Bob Jones

K12

ACE

Learn More:

I don't know of any books on this topic, since its goal is to replicate public school at home. Here are some bloggers who journal their experience with this:

ConfessionsofaHomeschooler.com

TheUnlikelyHomeschool.com

Which philosophy do I use? I'm definitely an eclectic homeschooler. My deeply-held beliefs on education work with several of the approaches detailed here. Passion-based learning is the bomb. Follow what your children love and let them guide their education and they'll learn deeply while learning to love learning.

We do lots of unit studies when they sound fun. We are part of a LEMI Commonwealth School (this is part of A Thomas Jefferson Education philosophy) because their teen projects/programs are incredibly impactful, and the parenting community is like balm for a thinking-woman's soul. I also mentor my children using TJED mentoring techniques. We sometimes use The Good and the Beautiful curriculum, but we skip parts that don't appeal to us and turn them into unit studies to make them more fun. There is an ebb and flow in how we do things that vacillates between TJED, Unschooling, Charlotte Mason, and Unit Studies. This might sound complicated, but it's actually how I make it simple for our family. For me, it's much easier to change gears and mix things up if it means I have happy, interested children engaged in learning at all times, rather than trying to force things when we're all feeling burned out.

My Learning Philosophy

*What are your beliefs about
parental stewardship?*

_____
_____
_____
_____
_____

*What is your belief about how children's
brains learn the best?*

_____
_____
_____
_____
_____

*What is your belief about how adult
brains learn the best?*

_____

_____

_____

_____

*What are your beliefs about educating the heart
alongside educating the mind?*

_____

_____

_____

_____

*What are your feelings about the greatest physical
environments for learning?*

_____

_____

_____

_____

What do you feel is the parent's role in educating children? (Direct instructor, formal teaching, tutor, child-led but parent guided, facilitator, mentor, assistant to a professional teacher, a mix of all of these, or other?)

_____
_____
_____
_____
_____
_____
_____
_____
_____
_____

How do you define a robust education?

_____
_____
_____
_____
_____

How does family culture fit in to getting a robust education?

_____
_____
_____
_____
_____

When is one's education complete?

_____
_____
_____
_____
_____

After thoughtfully journaling each of the above questions, summarize each answer into 1-2 succinct and clear sentences. Copy the sentences into a paragraph to create your personal education manifesto.

My Education Manifesto

6. Curriculum

Just kidding, I'm not going to write this chapter. If you haven't skipped any previous sections in this book, you probably already know I'm not going to tell you what curriculum to buy (or to download for free, as many are free.)

If you're looking for a place to start so that you have some structure to your day, start with a simple morning routine which includes a Morning Basket. This is a way for you to create a family curriculum and routine that rotates or changes over time, but has a set structure each day. I suggest starting with a prayer, a song, scriptures, and then add in other things that are important to your family. This could include poetry, folk songs, green smoothies, hot cocoa, fairy tales, board games, classic literature, affirmations, scripture recitations, the Pledge of Allegiance, journaling, a dance party, exercise… you get the idea. I accomplish this by way of a Morning Basket.

What's a Morning Basket? It's a basket filled with books and resources you want to draw from to inspire young minds. We start all of our days either cuddled up on the couch or in my bed or around the breakfast table reading and doing things from our Morning Basket.

Here is a sampling of what's usually in my Morning Basket:

- Scriptures
- Collection of folk tales and poetry from whichever country we are currently studying
- *Mathemagic* (This is an old book that is part of the Childcraft series. It makes math come alive for all ages. If you ever see one at a used book store, GET IT! If you see five, BUY THEM ALL! They make a most treasured gift.)
- Magazines published by our church which contain inspiring stories for children and teens.
- One of the books from Millennial Instructor (right now we are slowly working our way through their book called *The True Olive Tree*, but we have also loved their Bees book and Rocks book.
- Journals of our family's ancestors
- Our current read-aloud chapter book (usually a classic, with some newer books from time to time. I'm very picky about our longer read-aloud choices).
- I will also throw in things like picture books about certain holidays, seasons, or historical events we are honoring.

I don't read from all of these every morning, but we choose 3-5 things to read from each morning while I have a captive audience of groggy morning faces, or a captive audience of faces being fed breakfast. I love reading from our Morning Basket because it's a way for me to rotate through rich and beautiful literature, poetry, art and music before the day gets busy and full of energy.

The Morning Basket also creates the perfect segue into whatever else you want to accomplish that day. Everyone's already here, so at that point, you can transition right into any family learning, like history, science, or Unit Studies. Or, you can finish the Morning Basket and have everyone split off into independent rotations (one child on piano practice while another does math and yet another is working one-on-one with you on reading practice).

We choose to start every morning with scriptures, prayer, and a hymn. I can't describe how well this sets the tone for the rest of the day. There is a notable difference in the success of the days when we do this vs. when we don't. I believe and have seen continual proof that we learn everything best when the spirit is in our home and in our hearts. When we start the day with this, everything else goes more smoothly.

Regardless of whether you include any of the things I've mentioned, a morning routine is the key to a successful day. You can fill it with whatever your family values. As long as the morning routine happens, even if it's the *only* thing that happens that day, you will feel like you have accomplished something and fed your children's minds and souls.

Our Morning Routine

What are some habits, content, or media valued by your family that you want to start prioritizing on a regular basis? (Think outside the box of a morning routine and list all kinds of things you want to focus on regularly.)

_____
_____
_____
_____
_____
_____
_____
_____
_____
_____
_____
_____
_____
_____
_____
_____
_____
_____

_____
_____
_____
_____

Why do these things hold value for you? What do they add to your family's culture? How do they add beauty to your life or help you grow?

_____
_____
_____
_____
_____

Picture an ideal morning for your family. What adjectives describe the feeling in your home during this morning?

_____
_____
_____
_____
_____

How can the habits, content, and media from the previous page create the desired feelings in your home, and/or how can they create a cascading effect that breathes life into the rest of the day?

_____
_____
_____
_____
_____

Brainstorm ideas for things to put in your Morning Basket.

_____
_____
_____
_____
_____
_____
_____
_____
_____

*Brainstorm ideas to design
your morning routine*

7. Planning Your Year

Your learning philosophy/manifesto, your personality, and the state you live in will greatly dictate the things you do to plan your year. Regardless of those factors, it's a good idea to plan the broad strokes of your year first, then zoom in on your terms or months, and finally, create a weekly schedule to accomplish what you want. This can be as routine-oriented or as free-form as you wish it to be.

This section contains tips that can help every type of planner. First, let's talk about some factors that will influence how you plan, and how they may affect you personally.

Personality

A lot of prospective homeschoolers tell me they worry about their ability to be successful because they aren't really good at following rigid schedules. They worry they'll fall behind due to "laziness." The more people I talk to, the more I'm convinced that most people are this way to some degree. Most people label themselves as either lazy or undisciplined. But I wouldn't call it laziness. Our world today is so incredibly fast-paced and packed full of activities and routines, many people have forgotten the importance of slowing down and savoring the moment.

My theory is that the human heart craves connection to the lost art of slower living and savoring moments, yet we also see value in working hard and filling our schedules to the brim. We overfill our plates—just like everyone else—only to find it unsustainable. Then we swing the pendulum the other direction to gain "balance" in our lives. When that doesn't work, we blame our behavior on a character flaw called laziness or undisciplined.

But are you really either of those things? Or does your spirit just crave a different pace of life than the breakneck speed that has become today's "normal" lifestyle?

You are currently reading a book about taking back control of your child's entire education. You are not lazy. I have a few exciting and liberating pieces of news for you:

1. Your child can get the same amount of learning accomplished in three hours at home as s/he can in a week at school.

2. It doesn't matter if you "do school" from 8:00 a.m. to noon, or from 4:00 to 8:00 p.m., or for an hour in the morning and an hour in the evening, or to squeeze formal learning in wherever it fits, in between errands, extra curricular activities, jobs, or farm chores. Learning can take place just about any time or place.

3. You can do math in the car on the way to a 10:00 a.m. piano lesson and history as an audiobook on the way home.

4. You know how children go through physical growth spurts? They go through learning growth spurts, too. I've seen children who are "behind" in math hit a learning spurt and complete two years worth of math mastery in a month's time. I've seen children who are "behind" in reading go from only knowing half the alphabet sounds to reading beginner chapter books in a month. They can do this because their minds were ready.

Whether you are a master scheduler who loves routine, a spontaneous free-spirit, or anything in between, you can create a schedule or a rhythm that works for your family.

Where You Live

Where you live does determine somewhat how you need to schedule things. The Home School Legal Defense Association has a map you can click to view the homeschool laws in your state: https://hslda.org/legal

In some states, all you need to do is sign a homeschool affidavit at the local district office. You're on your own after that and can run your homeschool however you like. Other states have requirements such as keeping a log of all you do and taking attendance each day. I highly suggest you not only look up these rules, but also find other homeschoolers in your area to see how they meet these requirements. Oftentimes the written requirement seems daunting, but homeschool parents are inherently such resourceful problem-solvers. They will likely have come up with a very manageable way to meet all the requirements and will be happy to share it with you. Even in some of the more regulated states, it can be as simple as keeping a homeschool planner, writing down what you study each day, and having your children take a yearly skills assessment.

Your Learning Philosophy and Chosen Areas of Study

Start by deciding which subjects you would like to cover. This is going to vary based on your children's ages and your learning philosophy. For example, if you feel that younger children need no formal learning until a certain age, you might choose to include lots of reading, music, art, and nature for younger children, then add formal math, science, and writing for your older children.

If it's important for you to follow the subjects taught in public school, you may decide to include reading, writing, and math for your younger students, then add science and history as they get older.

Outline a general idea of what the "bones" of your curriculum will include.

Next, breathe some life into your school by filling in the gaps with passion projects and other things your family values. Is family history a passion of yours that you would like to pass on to your children? Participating in this activity can spill over into several school subjects, including reading, writing, history, geography, and social studies. Do you have a child who comes alive over art or music? Homeschooling allows ample time for them to delve deeply into these. Both art and music spill over into math and science. Does your family love to play board games? Introduce yourself to the world of game-schooling and see how playing certain games can help learning in every area imaginable.

> "THEY BELIEVE THAT EDUCATION IS SOMETHING THAT CHILDREN (AND PEOPLE OF ALL AGES) DO FOR THEMSELVES, NOT SOMETHING DONE TO THEM, AND THEY BELIEVE THAT EDUCATION IS A NORMAL PART OF ALL LIFE, NOT SOMETHING SEPARATE FROM LIFE THAT OCCURS AT SPECIAL TIMES IN SPECIAL PLACES."
>
> PETER GRAY, PSYCHOLOGY TODAY

Last but certainly not least, include your children and allow them to set their own goals. It's no fun for anyone when you're the only one pushing for your child to learn. If they're excited about something, they'll likely help to "push along" the learning. When they are excited about the topic, their learning becomes ignited. Even if your child comes up with the most random learning goal, it can likely be connected to (and even actively contribute to their progress in) a "school subject." Remember my beatboxing example from Chapter 2? Your children are brilliant. Trust that their interests, along with your guidance, will lead them down wonderful and exciting learning paths.

Add to your outline some goals, interests, and gifts your children have that you would like to foster and grow during the school year.

Turn to the subject planner sheets starting on page 150. Work with your children to plan ways they can align their interests and gifts with learning. You can compartmentalize your ideas into learning subjects, or write down integrative/general goals and objectives. <u>Only focus on the Subject and Method columns at this time. Leave the rest of the planner sheet blank.</u>

8. Tools for Planning Your Term, Unit, Month, or Week

Many homeschoolers like to take their yearly goals and break them down into terms or units. Whether you decide to do this depends on how "schedul-y" you want your school to be and how old your children are. If you do decide to plan a schedule for your term, remember that you get to make the rules. It doesn't have to look like a school schedule at all! Here are some great methods that many homeschool families enjoy.

Cycling

Following a cycle of time on/time off. It could be six weeks on, one week off. Or four weeks on, one week off. Or 12 weeks on, one week/month off. This is a popular schedule for those who utilize Unit Studies, as they will complete a full Unit Study during their 6 week period and then take a period of time off in preparation for the next Unit Study.

Some families end each six-week cycle with a celebration. One mom I know does 12-week cycles culminating in a "Battle of the Brains" day, which is full of games and friendly-competition where siblings show off what they've learned to each other and one child receives the Battle of the Brains trophy. Mom also throws a pizza party and anyone who completed their work for the term gets to attend the party. What a great way to celebrate and honor each other's progress and build family culture!

The week off is spent in preparation for the next term: Parents can prepare projects and activities for the next cycle, and children can work on passion projects. This cycling on and off is a great way to avoid burnout and fit in lots of family vacations, stay-cations, or camping trips. Another perk of homeschooling, you can do these fun and celebratory activities and trips at any time, not just during prescribed school breaks when the travel destinations are packed full of spring-breakers!

Course of Study

This method is probably most familiar because it resembles public school. It utilizes a basic lesson plan book that you can buy at any office supply store. Parents who use this type of schedule simply decide how often each subject will be done and add them to their weekly lesson plans, filling in the blocks. For example, math could be done daily, grammar three times a week, history twice a week, and science two days a week. Using your lesson planner, write down the assignments and any necessary notes.

Though I do not schedule our learning in this way, I still utilize this type of planner in a backwards way. I use it as a journal to write in what we have *done* each day, rather than what we *plan to do* each day. I'll cover this in more detail later.

Looping

A loop schedule is simply a list of subjects or activities that you work through for a set amount of time. When the time is up, you stop. When you start working again (whether it's later that day or the next day, or the next week if you're taking a break) you begin where you left off. When you complete the list, you move back to the top and repeat—making a loop. You can use a loop schedule for all your subjects, a specific group of subjects, or whatever method works for you.

Some families use a loop schedule for all the extras they want to fit in. For example, each child is assigned reading, writing, and math each day, but there is also a family loop schedule to include fun things like art projects, music, poetry, museum trips, etc. Every day after finishing skill subjects, they begin working on the next item in their loop. After completing that, if time allows, they move to the next item on the list. It doesn't matter which day of the week it is, you just continue "looping" through the list. This way, even though skill subjects take priority, you're still able to fit in the enjoyable content subjects that we like so much.

I utilize looping in different ways. Each of my older children, who are working on bigger learning projects, have a personal loop they work through. For example, last year, my oldest son was participating in a lot of intense classes. He was in a Shakespeare Scholar class which required a lot of reading, memorizing, and writing. He was in an oceanography study group with weekly meet-ups and an end-of-year sailing trip on a 1700s style brigantine ship. He was also taking a certification class to become a drone pilot and was in an advanced math tutoring group. At an age where it's hard to keep track of lots of spinning plates, he relied a lot on his loop to keep him always working toward his goals, but almost never feeling like he was getting behind or dropping the ball on any projects.

By looping, he was able to allot a certain amount of time each day to his studies. If one math concept took him longer to learn than others, that was okay. He knew there was a dedicated block of time to work on it several times a week, and that going at his own pace is okay. Being able to honor the way his brain works, slowing down when he needed and speeding up when he was able, was a huge confidence-builder for him. He succeeded in all of these classes and was able to meet all of his deadlines without feeling the need to keep up with his peers or stay back with his peers. It created a very healthy balance of accomplishment and rest, something that many teenagers have a hard time finding.

In addition to my older kids using a loop, I also use a family loop that works well with our daily and weekly schedule, which I prefer to call a rhythm rather than a schedule, simply because when I tell myself it's a schedule, my brain quickly attempts to rebel, and within a few days, I feel like a failure. But you can't fail a rhythm!

Because looping works so well for my family and I've mentored many homeschoolers through implementing it with their unique learning philosophy, I created a video tutorial and a way for you to custom-create your own looping system and print it. It's a free gift for my homeschool community and you can find it by going to www.HappyAtHomeschool.com and clicking on Resources. I recommend watching the video, regardless of which system you use to plan your homeschool, as there are lots of little tips and insights that can be applied in multiple settings.

Block Scheduling

A block schedule uses blocks of time to focus on a specific subject. It can be as long as a term or quarter, or as short as a week or two. Here's an example of a short block: instead of scheduling history for three days a week and science for the other two days, you could choose to

> "Where are the writing lessons you may ask? Where is the college prep? It's everywhere! Instead of reading a dozen or more assigned books, your children are likely to have read hundreds. That's how Jefferson, Scott, Stowe, Stevenson and Tolstoy learned. And as your children read, they will have pondered and asked their own questions. Their minds will be filled with ideas and their hearts will be full of desire. The secret of their success will not be in how many things they know about, but in how many things they care about. And they'll care about a lot of things."
>
> Marlene Peterson

focus on history for a full week or two (or even a term) before shifting focus to science. You can plan all your subjects according to blocks or use a block schedule for only certain subjects, combining this type of schedule with another format. It works very well for families that like to dive deep into a subject. I have successfully used this to rotate back and forth between science and history, while still including basics like math and reading every day.

Checklists

Probably the most simple method, but still quite effective, is a daily or weekly checklist. All you need is a notebook and a pencil. Write down the projects you want your child to spend time on for the day (assignments, if you want to call them that), and let your child check them off as they are completed.

This is a great method for middle school and high school, when they are working more independently. Teach them to write the assignments down and cross them off as they are completed. My teenager seems to be moving into a phase where he thrives on the checklist method. Each morning, we have a meeting to discuss his goals for the day (while looking ahead at his goals for the week and the month), and he writes his own checklist into his planner.

He has really taken to checking his planner throughout the day. It makes him feel independent and capable of planning and executing his daily life. But had I introduced this method to him even one or two years ago, there would have been a lot of aversion to it and may have soured his view of using a planner for life! Checklists can be liberating for some and feel like jail for others, so use it judiciously.

Family Rhythm

Many new homeschoolers try to recreate a public school regimen in a home based setting. This is not only difficult to achieve, but also prevents a lot of the wonderful aspects of homeschooling from occurring. Instead of a rigid schedule, I created a Family Rhythm. I love it because it's flexible and facilitates open-ended learning with plenty of "downtime" for exploring and creating. It also keeps the whole family apprised on what's coming up in the week and ensures we don't miss anything important.

We all need at least a little bit of routine and structure in life, and this is the perfect level of routine for my free-spirited heart. I feel successful as a mom when I follow this rhythm rather than a "schedule," which always feels more rigid to me. I created a video tutorial and a way for you to custom-create your own Family Rhythm system and print it. It's a free gift for my homeschool community and you can find it by going to www.HappyAtHomeschool.com and clicking on Resources. I recommend watching the video regardless of which system you use to plan your homeschool, as this tool, like looping, can be applied to many different situations.

Brainstorm ideas on how you will go about planning your year, terms/units/months.

9. Structuring Each Day

This is the daunting part for most new homeschoolers. Until you're doing it day-to-day, it's difficult to envision how in the world you will get through every school subject for several children who are all in different age groups, while still running the household, keeping everyone fed and clothed, *and* somehow still have time to also be a normal human with her/his own needs, interests, career, etc. Without being able to see how this can work, it's easy for anyone to envision a rapid path toward burnout.

Deep breath.

Here's how it's possible.

There are many things that the public school system does out of necessity, in order to manage large classrooms of children. Some of these things are having seven-hour school days, compartmentalizing information and knowledge into "subjects," and segregating children by age. None of these things are necessary in a home setting, nor are most of them effective when you're learning in small groups like a family. I'm going to touch on each one, so exhale that deep breath you just sucked in a minute ago.

Seven Hour School Days

Long school days at home are not necessary for adequate, or even advanced, learning to take place. Children spend on average 7 hours a day in school. But not all of this is direct instruction time. After you subtract time for lunch, recess (or 5 minutes between each period for middle- and high-schoolers), lining up and standing in line, waiting for 30 kids to switch modes from one task to the next, interruptions from chatty and distracting students, days in which teachers play movies to fill time, school assemblies and school spirit activities, there is not a ton of time left for actual core instruction.

There have been several surveys and assessments done to distill the school day down to how many instructional hours are taking place. I averaged the results of these studies and it appears that only 12 hours per week of direct learning in core subjects is occurring in grades 1 through12.

So what does this mean for homeschool? Since virtually none of those things need to be subtracted from your learning time, you can very likely keep up with what the school system is doing as long as you spend at least 2.4 hours per week-day concentrated on learning.

But wait, there's more! Don't forget that those 12 hours per week are still spent in classes of 20 to 35 students. Can this be more efficient if you are working one-on-one with your child? Now factor in your ability to teach your child in a way that he/she learns best, rather than how it's easiest to teach in a large group setting. Can you be even more efficient?

I'm not advocating for a 30 minute school day, but hopefully I'm successfully illustrating how an hour here and an hour there can add up to a lot of *formal* learning. If you create a family culture of constant learning (we say, "We're never not learning!"), then *informal* learning can take place every minute of the day.

Compartmentalizing Knowledge Into Subjects

Another thing that happens in public schools is compartmentalized learning. While there's nothing wrong with that, it's also true that knowledge and learning don't really have clear delineations. They bleed together in beautiful and interesting ways. Can you see how math is also art? Literature is also history. History is also home economics. Baking is also science. Science is also math. Math is also music. Music is also humanities. Making these important connections turns facts into knowledge and knowledge into wisdom.

You can take this to whatever extreme you feel comfortable with, but even very conservatively, you can often "kill two birds with one stone." This is one of the reasons many families love Unit Study. It not only helps children make connections between what they're learning and the world around them, it also provides a simple way to teach several subjects at once. Understanding this concept and seeing it work in practice helps take the pressure off of us to "Do history class from 9:00 a.m. to 10:00 a.m. Do language arts from 10:00 am. to 11:00 a.m." (Picture me making robot arm motions as I say that.)

Teaching Multiple Ages

This is one of my favorite aspects of homeschooling. Long ago, at the onset of the very first standardized schoolhouses in America, all the school-aged children met in the same room. It was called a one-room schoolhouse. First graders learned alongside 6th graders and everyone in between. I imagine in some ways it was chaotic, but a lot of really awesome things were happening, too.

Learning together with your siblings or friends of different ages allows younger children to have mentors to look up to in their older peers. An older child tutoring a younger one enriches their own learning and teaches them empathy. There are so many layers of benefits to allowing children of all ages to learn together and bring their different perspectives to the table.

Of course, some subjects need to be taught by level. Reading must, of course, be taught or guided at the level of each child. We spend lots of one-on-one time with children when they are first learning to read. But once they are independently reading, you don't need to teach them how to read ever again! Huzzah! From there,

> "THE HOME IS THE FIRST AND MOST EFFECTIVE PLACE TO LEARN THE LESSONS OF LIFE: TRUTH, HONOR, VIRTUE, SELF CONTROL, THE VALUE OF EDUCATION, HONEST WORK, AND THE PURPOSE AND PRIVILEGE OF LIFE. NOTHING CAN TAKE THE PLACE OF HOME IN REARING AND TEACHING CHILDREN, AND NO OTHER SUCCESS CAN COMPENSATE FOR FAILURE IN THE HOME."
>
> DAVID O. MCKAY

"reading class" is about giving them access to lots of living books and beautiful literature. (A living book is a non-fiction book written by someone who has a deep passion for the subject and writes in a way that makes that subject come alive for the reader. I hope this book comes across as a living book about homeschooling.)

Math, of course, needs to be learned line-upon-line, each concept building upon the last. So in math, there is some one-on-one time needed.

Topics that need a little (or a lot of) one-on-one time, I set on a rotation so that I'm working with one child while their siblings are doing independent work. For example, one child might be taking their turn practicing the piano and another is working through math problems independently, while I am working individually with another child on learning to read. When that reading lesson is over, I'm now open for individual work with another child. One might come to me with math help while the second child is taking their turn on the piano, and a third child is playing with legos or play-doh. A half hour later, I might have two children in their rooms reading independently while I'm helping my youngest with her violin practice.

I have a friend who has more children than I do, and she designates a math time wherein everyone sits around the table and works. She also works on her own projects at the table but is available for any interruptions in case someone needs help with a math problem. Independent work vs. work that needs attentive parental help is something that you'll likely need to guess at until you fall into a groove. Just stay the course and try different things until something clicks into place.

I've talked about how reading and math need to be taught or learned by level. But virtually everything else, in my opinion and experience, can successfully and joyfully be taught in a "one-room schoolhouse," or as many people call it, "family school." We do family school for many subjects. We make it fun and exciting and I teach with living books, great videos, and hands-on projects and experiments. We are all learning together, including me. I "teach" or direct our explorations to the level of my oldest child. The younger children absorb exactly what they are ready to absorb, at their own level. Too often, we dumb-down information because we assume that younger children won't comprehend. But aren't they constantly surprising us since toddlerhood with just how much they are able to understand?

In a history lesson about ancient Egypt, I might have a coloring page for younger children which depicts some aspect of living long ago near the Nile river. My youngest colors it and plays with playdoh while she listens to me read a living book or historical fiction to everyone. The older kids might draw or write in their journals about what they're learning. Together, we might do a craft, making jeweled gold wrist-cuffs like they wore in the time of Cleopatra. My oldest, who doesn't love crafts, will read a passage I found for him that is more advanced and in-depth on the subject, and then come and discuss it with me while the rest of us finish up the craft. Then we watch a movie together about how gold was forged anciently to make jewelry in contrast to how it is used in modern day. This is what a History Unit Study might look like. But see how it has covered not only history, but also literature, writing and penmanship practice, and science?

You can teach parts of speech and grammar, science, history, art, and more in a family-school setting.

Another powerful benefit of teaching multiple-aged children at once is the opportunity they have to help their younger siblings. As your children age, older children can help younger children with spelling, math, educational board games, etc. Have you noticed that when you teach someone something, it deepens your own understanding of that topic? In order to teach someone, your brain goes through a process of reorganizing the information to get ready to explain it to someone who doesn't know as much. This creates new neural pathways for that information to travel in the brain. When your older child teaches a younger child something–anything–they solidify their own knowledge in meaningful ways. Don't even get me started on the sibling connections that are made when a big brother or sister kindly shows their sibling how to do something! It melts a mama's heart.

Putting It All Together

Only you can create the "perfect" (perfectly imperfect, mind you) homeschool regimen for your family. It still helps to have living examples, so I'll share with you our typical day. I'm going to put times of day next to these activities, but this is only for purposes of showing you how our day progresses. It's not a schedule and we don't use timers to let us know that math time is over. It's a rhythm that fluctuates based on the season, family events and projects, and ages of my children.

Monday, Tuesday, and Wednesday

- 6:30: I wake up and exercise, read scriptures, journal, meditate, start breakfast

- 7:30-8:00: Family begins to wake up and wander down for breakfast

- 8:00: Eat breakfast, morning routine, Morning Basket, clean up breakfast

- ***Break for chores. (We follow my Agency-Based Chores system which you can find at HappyatHomeschool.com) I also start a load of laundry and shower if I didn't get to it earlier

- 10:00: Family Loop. Everything on our family loop is family-school style (learning together, rather than independently). We usually rotate between science, history and art (art being art history, visual art, poetry, literature and performing arts), but sometimes I'll throw other things in as needed, like an internet safety course or learning how to do family history/indexing.

- 12:00: Lunch and outside time.

- 12:30 or 1:00: Rotations. (This is where each child gets through the rest of their independent learning goals for the day with or without my help. They rotate having one-on-one time with me while the others do independent work. One of my children does their math completely independent of me and I just check problems with them when they're done to see if we need to figure something out. Another child needs me to walk through his math with him, problem by problem so math is usually his one-on-one time. I work with him while his older brother does math and his younger sister reads. Then we rotate until everyone's done.) My teenager also uses his rotation time to login to classes he's taking online. This year, he took several community and

> "EDUCATION IS NOT THE FILLING OF A PAIL, BUT THE LIGHTING OF A FIRE."
>
> WILLIAM BUTLER YEATS

online classes. He didn't need my help with any of it because teenagers are *amazing*.

- Some days I am needed for one-on-one during rotation time much more than others. But sometimes, the math chapter they're on is something they're grasping on their own, so I can start prepping dinner, answer emails, read something I enjoy, work on a project, write a book about homeschooling… and I just make myself available for interruptions.

- 1:30 or 2:00, depending on the day: Everyone puts away school books and supplies and has free time for the remainder of the afternoon. Outside play, friend time, passion projects, etc.

- At dinner, we often discuss what we learned during the day to bring Dad into the loop. This reinforces learning and sometimes the discussions are exploratory and fun. After dinner, we work on family projects, go on outings, play board games together, play outside together, etc. I consider all of this passive learning time, but we are *never not learning!*

Thursday

Thursdays we attend our commonwealth school. It's a group of about 30 other families who have become an extension of our family. My kids' best friends are there. Their mothers are my best friends. This school and these relationships breathe life into me and recharge my homeschooling heart.

The moms teach classes, and we have a rotation set up so that there is even a one-hour moms class. During mom's class (this year it's my turn to teach this class), we discuss all sorts of beautiful things. We have book colloquiums, we philosophize about everything under the sun, we edify and uplift each other, we share tips on parenting, meal planning, relationships, entrepreneurship, and more. It's a lot of work to keep it running, but everyone there agrees that it's fulfilling work, and worth every minute of our careful planning.

I highly suggest you find or create a group like this, whether it's joining a commonwealth, joining a co-op, or putting together a mothers group of like-minded women who meet regularly to inspire each other while the children play. You're going to need a community who "gets" you and who can "sing the song of your heart when you forget the tune." In a way, since you're reading this, I get to be part of your community. I am honored to do so! Make it a priority to find intentional, thinking women and families to create a supportive community. It will make all of your life easier!

Friday

As long as the rest of the week went fairly in accordance with our rhythm, we leave Fridays as an extension of our weekend. We hike, go on camping trips, stay-cations, museum trips, play dates, family projects, spring cleaning, or my favorite: just letting the children have free time while I garden, read, start a project (I'm always starting projects which I sometimes finish), make music, go get my hair done, have lunch with a friend, or write books about homeschooling. If we had a week full of disruptions to our rhythm, we will often use this Friday to catch up on some of the work and activities we missed earlier in the week.

Exceptions

We fit in things like violin lessons, gymnastics, and other classes into our week, too. Drive time is not wasted time. Almost everything we do in our school day can be done in the car. Audiobooks are used while traveling to and from activities. My kids sometimes bring their math books or reading books to work on while we drive.

Other exceptions include illness, vacations, holidays, and burnout. Let these things happen without worry of getting behind. You cannot prevent your children from learning.

Honestly? There are some days in the dead of winter where my morning routine before the family wakes up does not happen. So rather than everyone waking up to the sounds of me making breakfast while listening to my favorite podcast, they'll wake up and slowly gather in my bed. One of them will drag our morning basket in and I'll sit up in bed and read to them. Sometimes this leads to getting out of bed and having a really productive day. Sometimes it leads to everyone getting ready for the day and then crawling back into my bed with cocoa and popcorn and we have a blessed day of documentaries. Hallelujah!

Very routine-oriented readers might think this silly, but I hope that all you free-spirits out there take heart. I'm fairly confident my adult children will look back on our "hygge" days with a whole lot of cozy nostalgia.

Turn to page 150 and add to your subject planner sheets by filling in the Logistics and Frequency columns. Indicate for each area of study how you plan to learn (family-school style, in rotations, on a loop, one-on-one work, daily independent work or any other method you invent). Also indicate how often you want to spend time in each area of study.

10. Mom Care: How to Survive and Thrive

There is a big self-care movement happening right now, and I'm in full support of it. Women are finally being given the permission to take care of themselves. But the "how" is important—and I've noticed some problems in the messaging of how women (specifically) are being told to implement that self care. I'm constantly seeing messages on how to "treat yourself" in ways that are a counterfeit to real self care.

You're probably familiar with the safety instructions repeated every time you fly in an airplane. One of the instructions given is that if oxygen masks drop, you are to put your mask on first before you help your children or those around you. This is important because if you pass out, you can't help anybody around you. It's okay if your child passes out for a couple of seconds as long as you are able to get that mask on them quickly so they can recover their oxygen levels. But if *you* pass out, there will likely be no one to help your child. There are many layers of analogy here. Put your mask on first.

As often as possible, remain the best, or at least a functioning, version of yourself so you can have a greater impact in your home, family, community, and world.

Putting your mask on first is not selfish, it's productive. Rest and down time is productive. When we're burned out, we are incapable of living intentionally. When we're completely tapped, our prefrontal cortex, which uses logic and empathy to solve problems, takes a back seat and our limbic brain takes the driver's seat. This is our fight, flight, or freeze brain. When our limbic system is driving, we can't intentionally create a good atmosphere or connection with our loved ones. We're in complete survival mode.

How do we get into survival mode? My experience is that it's usually because I have allowed myself to believe that I can't take a break and put myself first because it would be selfish. So I burn both ends of the candle until I'm forced to take a break because I'm so depleted.

Break down the word selfish into SELF-ish, and you can see that it is a focus on self. When I get into a mode where my self talk sounds like, "*I* can't take a break. *I* have so much to do. Everyone needs *me*. It's all on *my* shoulders. *I* have to take care of everyone. *I* have to dig us out of this situation." Do you notice how many times I thought the word "I" and "me"? The focus is on my*self*. Rather than self-care being selfish, consider the possibility that sometimes *not* taking self-care is the selfish thing.

Still, we feel…selfish. Am I right? But I think we feel this way because of counterfeit selfcare.

The counterfeit is how the world tells us to take our "me" time: Go shopping, "treat yo'self", eat junk food, get a pedicure, go to the spa, get a spray tan, go out with the girls. None of these things are bad, and none of them have to be selfish. But ask your heart of hearts, do those things truly recharge my batteries, or are they a temporary fix? Are they self *care*, or are they self *indulgence*?

I'm not saying that *you* are self indulgent if you choose any of the activities above. I have done all of the things on that list. What I'm suggesting is that if you're using these and other things as self care, and are constantly feeling like you need more and more self care to keep your batteries charged, maybe the things you've been told are self care are not really self care. They're just fun indulgences.

People often say they can't do proper self care because they don't have it in the budget. Again, that's because we've been told that we need a $7 bath bomb, a $30 pedicure, and a trip to the ice cream store in order to participate in self care.

I often find myself "taking a break" from my day to scroll social media on my phone. My break ends up being longer than I realized, and yet my brain doesn't feel like I got a break. It doesn't recharge my batteries. Instead, it saps them even further, because our brains get inundated with excess stimuli and incoming information when we use social media.

So what types of self care activities result in actually caring for ourselves? What will recharge our brain's batteries and make us feel whole again? Only you can answer that question. What are some things that use your brain in invigorating and exciting ways? Reading an awesome book? Participating in a hobby? Writing? Being in nature? You will find specific things that align with your personal gifts and interests.

Self Care Myths and Truths

Myth: Self care is indulgent.

Truth: Meaningful self care includes making mindful changes in patterns of thoughts and behaviors that do not contribute to your wellbeing.

Myth: Self care is selfish.

Truth: When you make time for yourself and get sufficient rest and exercise, you feel more energetic and will be able to do more for yourself as well as for those around you.

Myth: Self care is a one-time experience.

Truth: Looking after yourself is an ongoing practice that helps build resilience in the face of hardships and prevents burnout.

Myth: Self care is time-consuming.

Truth: If you're doing the right things, self care does not require a huge chunk of time from your busy day.

Here a few self-care activities that work for absolutely everyone:

- Creating and eating a healthy meal

- Drinking enough water

- Getting enough sleep

- Exercising

- Standing barefoot in the grass

- Meditation

- Taking the supplements your body needs

- Reading scriptures or other uplifting text

- Praying

- Being with your tribe. (Read more about this in the next section about mothers groups.)

Self Care:

- Leaves you feeling nourished
- May be hard to do at first
- Regular and consistent
- Addresses core needs
- Builds you up

Self-Indulgence

- Leaves you feeling depleted
- Associated with feelings of guilt or shame
- Happens inconsistently
- Doesn't address underlying needs
- Costs you (money, health, character, etc.)

How to Find "Me" Time When You Homeschool

How do you find the time to care for yourself when you homeschool? I'm going to explain a few ways. Ponder each of them and consider whether they'll work for you. Better yet, give each of them a concerted effort, because they might surprise you!

It feels difficult, and sometimes impossible, to take time away from what's already being spent on managing a home, caring for children, working, homeschooling, etc. So rather than *taking* time away from the day, look into ways you can *create more* time in your day. Inventory your life and see where you can create more time. Two glaringly obvious places I found in my life were:

1. The screen-time report my phone likes to send me every week sometimes causes me to feel shame (there's a red flag that too much social media time for me becomes self-indulgence rather than self-care). If I were to cease and desist my idle phone usage, it would free up a lot of time in my life. I had a choice: keep on as I had been, or take a leap of faith and set some social media boundaries so that I could use that time intentionally to put on my oxygen mask.

2. I could create more time in my day by waking up earlier and going to bed earlier. STOP! Don't close the book! Hear me out because, sister, I am *not* a morning person and I relish sleeping in as often as possible. I read a book called *Miracle Morning* by Hal Elrod. It is short, simple, and life-changing. I recommend reading it to develop your own Miracle Morning routine, but the gist of it is to carve out intentional morning time to:

    - Sit in silent contemplation
    - Visualize or meditate
    - Exercise
    - Read and study from your core books
    - Write (anything–traditional journaling, stream of consciousness, to do lists, etc.)

I hate waking up even one minute earlier than my body decides is a joyful and comfortable time to get out of bed. But I gave this a whirl (knowing I would feel tired the first week until I adjusted) and it changed my life. Some mornings I can fit in a 40 minute workout and an hour of study, journaling, and prayer. Some mornings, I spend just one minute on each of these, for a total of a 5-minute Miracle Morning. Of course the longer time offers me more sanctification and centering. But even with my tiny 5-minute mornings, I have an entire day that is more focused, productive, peaceful, and fulfilling.

It means I also go to bed earlier, yes. So how does this create more time? Two reasons: I don't know about you, but my "need" to stay up late comes from my feeling like I didn't get enough done during the day, and now that my littles are finally asleep, it's my only chance to get some things done and have some quiet time. The only problem is, by the time my children are in bed, I'm spent! I'm not getting much quality work done. I'm spinning my wheels. It's inefficient at best and a useless waste at worst. If I transfer that time to the morning, I'm able to create so much more of an impact in my life, even though I'm tired when I first wake up. It's a different type of "tired."

Starting my day with a Miracle Morning creates even more time in the day because it creates so much momentum! I often find that I burn through my to-do list and take much fewer social media breaks because my brain doesn't crave them when I start my day this way. Please try this!

Some other ways to get quality self-care time:

- As your children get older, they will begin to notice your need for alone time and they will respect it. When I need alone time, I ask for it, and they usually give it to me.

- Institute a daily quiet time where everyone goes to a quiet place to read, write, draw, nap, or think. It's good for all, not just you.

- Join a co-op or a commonwealth school. Take the time to find one with a community in which you can feel completely at home being yourself.

- One way to avoid burnout in homeschool is to include things that you love in your curriculum. If you're an artist, add art to your curriculum. If you love nature, add family hikes to your school day. If you love baking, make it a part of your math, science, literature, and history.

- If you want your children to love learning, be the person who loves learning! Let your children see you dive into a new hobby. Let them see you start a business. Let them see you fail at it and try again. Let them see your curiosity pique at the thought of not knowing something, and then go find it out together. Show them how learning is not just a means to an end, it's a delicious process of discovery and adventure.

- Join or create a mother's group. Not just people who are geographically or relationally convenient, not just your default people, but a group of people that you curate into your life because they inspire you to grow and cause you to think in new and positive ways that you wouldn't otherwise. They curate you into their life because you bring the same value to them. If you do not have these people, it's time to start praying them into your life. I bet they're praying for you to come into theirs, too.

- If household chores are one of the things draining you, I highly recommend you listen to my audio course called Agency-Based Chores. It is a complete system that breathes life into a typical chore chart and inspires children to contribute because they want to, not because they're being forced. Having a mostly-organized and mostly-clean home at any given time removes a lot of mind-clutter, which contributes so much to mental overwhelm and burnout. For more information, visit happyathomeschool.com/chores/

Be sure to consider your season of life. When you have a newborn, it's not always feasible to wake up really early every day. When your children are really young and you don't have a teenager at home to help, you probably won't be planning regular lunch dates outside your home.

However you decide to self care for your circumstance, the bottom line is this: Start taking an inventory of the little breaks you're taking throughout the day. How are you currently doing self care?

Pay attention to how you feel when you're done with those breaks and those self-care efforts. If you still feel frazzled, drained, or resentful shortly afterward, then what you did during that break was not effective self care.

How to Make Your Daily Monotony Feel Like Self Care

Once upon a time, my life was burning me out on such a frequent basis that I felt like I could never, ever get enough "me" time to refill my bucket. It took me a long time to wake up and realize–wait a minute–This is MY life. If I have created something that I feel a need to constantly escape, something is wrong. How can I recreate my life into something that I don't feel the need to escape from?

If you're sarcastic like me, you might be thinking, "Welp? I guess I need to quit being a mom and run away, and make it all about me!" But I want you to think, if you are a mom—and you probably are if you're reading this—is there a way that being with your children can also be your "me" time? Not 100% of your "me" time, but can it be part of it?

We women wear so many hats, it's nauseating. When I'm with my children and wearing my homeschool-mom hat, my brain is sometimes elsewhere. The voices in my head are nagging, "Oh, man, I need a break! Oh man, I have all this stuff on my to do list, but I can't do it because these other humans need me so bad. Oh my gosh, it's time to make another meal and I feel like I just cleaned up the last one, why does everyone need to eat all the time? When is it going to be MY TURN!?"

When I'm in that headspace, it absolutely drains me. It makes me feel like I need to escape and take more "me" time. But if I make a conscious choice to wear only one hat at a time, whenever possible, and cut out everything else—remove my to do list from my brain, knowing I can come back to it later; delete all the thoughts of the things that my children are distracting me from and choose to go 100%, all in, fully present with them—something changes. I start zooming in on the details of the moment: zooming in on their chubby little hands or their eyelashes or the timbre of their cute little voices or the smell of their (endearingly) stinky hair from playing outside in the sun… There is nothing more fulfilling or recharging for a mother than when she *allows* herself to be fully present with her children.

For me, it's all about presence. When I can pull all of my thoughts to the present moment, not reflecting on the past, not worrying about the future, but 100% here, now, suddenly I feel no need to escape. The sound of my child's laughter fills up all the cracks and loosens all the gnarled places in my heart. I don't want to be anywhere else but here—my happy place.

Presence can also transform other areas of life. After my children have gone to bed and I'm doing the dishes, I sometimes find myself in the headspace of, "I'm working so hard, I never get a break, these dishes are always mounting…" But if I stop languishing there, and instead I put on a great podcast or some beautiful music, doing the dishes turns into a meditation instead of a chore.

Zoom in on the details. The smell of the soap, the feel of the warm water on my hands, the repetitive ritual of swirling your sponge around and around on a plate until it's clean. Am I sounding loony yet? I know, I know. But sometimes you just have to do the dishes. If the only choices are to do them while hating every moment or getting a little loony and turning it into a meditation, I choose loony every time. Make your daily redundant tasks into a meditation. It's magic.

The reason we need self care isn't so that we can look good while we socialize. We need it for our hearts and our minds. Becoming present gives us that. Becoming present with my children gives me that at an indescribably fulfilling level. In those moments, I remember that my kids aren't the distraction. Everything else is the distraction. These relationships are the most important things and the most fulfilling things, if I can only allow them to be.

Before you go thinking that I'm one of those moms who naturally gets so much joy and fulfillment out of mothering that I couldn't possibly ever want or need anything else—I am not. I have always run a business while mothering. I have always had hobbies and close friends while mothering. I sing in a professional choir which rehearses three hours a week and performs several concerts a year. I occasionally accept small contracts to go to the studio to record music. I go on walks with friends. I have an impactful mother's group that meets often to discuss non-surfacy things and fill each other up with light. As I write this, I'm thinking, "Wow, I really do a lot of things, and I haven't even started listing my other hobbies like painting, crocheting, gardening, etc." Mothering and homeschooling can fill my heart with joy, *and* I need these other things, too.

It will take some prioritizing and discipline to charge your batteries with real fuel, as opposed to quick fixes that don't last long, but as you keep refining your habits and cultivating a supportive community in your life, you will find that you can feel like a fulfilled, whole, multi-faceted human who also happens to be a homeschooling parent.

My Surviving and Thriving Plan

What are some things that make you feel completely drained?

_____
_____
_____
_____
_____

Could a new approach or outlook on these things help me feel less drained, or are they simply not beneficial in any way?

_____
_____
_____
_____
_____
_____
_____
_____
_____

What are some things I've been using as self care that aren't actually self care?

_____
_____
_____
_____
_____
_____
_____

What are some things I need to cease or reduce to free up time for true self care?

_____
_____
_____
_____
_____
_____
_____
_____
_____
_____
_____

What are some things that will recharge my batteries and provide me with real self care?

_____
_____
_____
_____
_____
_____
_____
_____

Brainstorm ideas for activities you would like to include in your personal morning routine.

_____
_____
_____
_____
_____
_____
_____
_____

Add some detail to each activity you wrote down. For example, what will you read? What will you listen to? How will you move your body? Where will you sit to read, journal, and plan the priorities of your day?

11. Ten Homeschooling Myths

The following are all lies that we have been fed for so long that most people don't even question them. But there is an awakening happening as people begin to realize that the common way is not the only effective way. I'll never tell someone that they "should" homeschool, even though I believe that every child can thrive in homeschool, provided they're receiving everything else required for thriving (a safe home with food, clothing, and love).

Homeschooling is not a new experiment. Mothers have taught their children since the beginning of time. It's public school that is the new experiment in society. It's only been about 200 years that we have passed education on to experts and begun to believe that we are unqualified. However, having experts teach our children has not resulted in statistically more educated humans—especially not if you consider the full effect of generational learning. (Collective knowledge of the world is carried forward to the next generation. If the new generation doesn't have to waste their time reinventing the wheel, they can focus on other things, like building rockets or curing cancer.) It's time to take back our families.

Let's dive into the most common myths about homeschooling. Hopefully these perspectives squash any fears you may be having.

Myth #1:
"Homeschooled children aren't socialized."

This is one of the top concerns that non-homeschoolers have about homeschooling, but it's not even real. Most people haven't even considered what the word "socialization" means, and when they do, they realize everyone has a different definition. Still, I had the same concern when I was looking into homeschooling. I'll never forget this conversation I had with a friend, who helped open my eyes:

"I'm worried about socialization."

"What's socialization?"

"You know, like my children getting plenty of social time with their peers instead of being isolated from them."

"Wait, they're allowed to do that at school!?"

"Well, not during class, of course, but yes."

"So you're worried about replacing 15 minutes of recess?"

You've got to love friends who talk straight to you. What I experienced after taking the leap to homeschool is that my children get far more play time with friends than they did when they were in public school. But it is more complicated than friend time, isn't it?

Parents are a child's first socializers. They're the determining factor for weirdness, kindness, manners, and more. If a parent is kind and generous, the child mostly likely will be that way, too. If a parent is foul-mouthed or racist, the child will likely be, too.

When children move on to public school, their peers and teachers take the place of parents as the foremost influencers of socializing. Many strong, courageous children have been turned shy due to bullying in school. Many honest children have learned to lie at school. Conversely, some children may witness their first examples of empathy and kindness in school, which they unfortunately didn't receive in their early years.

When someone asks me about socialization, I ask them to consider their own experiences in public school—what good character traits did they learn? What bad? Were they bullied? Was school a safe place for them—physically and emotionally?

You can take the time to journal these if you like, but often, clarity of your beliefs on socialization can come with just a few moments of thought on these questions:

1. What *is* socialization?
2. Describe a socially healthy person.
3. Does public school help create socially healthy people?
4. What good character traits have you learned in life? Did you learn them at school or at home?
5. What bad character traits have you learned in life?

Did you learn them at school or at home?

6. Have you ever met a freakishly weird public schooler? Are they weird in spite of school?

7. Have you ever met an impressively social and well-adjusted homeschooler? Are they amazing in spite of homeschooling?

8. Are people being socially healthy or not socially healthy based on how they are educated?

9. How can I best support my child in becoming a socially healthy person?

Myth #2:
"Homeschooling is expensive."

Homeschool can be massively expensive, completely free, or anywhere in between. All you truly need are lots of books and art supplies. Everything else is a bonus, including purchased curricula. With time and a library card, you really can teach your child everything.

There are so many free (or nearly free) resources that will allow you to meet most of your child's learning needs:

- A library card (for lots of books, videos, computer time, and other learning resource kits; free in most cities or a minimal fee to access a larger library)

- Online learning websites (Khan Academy online teaches math for free)

- Free curricula or curriculum swaps

- Trading skills, resources, tips and other helps with your local homeschool community

- Books and other supplies from the local thrift store or yard sales

- Back-to-school sales (stock up!)

- Museum passes (you can call museums and ask for education field trip discounts and get into most places for free or a discount)

- Lots of outside time to learn from nature and play

Some of the extras we've budgeted for (but that aren't completely necessary) are:

- Computer or tablet

- Educational board games (look up Gameschooling on the internet for so many suggestions)

- Bookshelves for all the books. Like *so* many books.

- Laminator (I use this a surprising amount)

- Bluetooth color printer (printing from your phone is life-changing)

- Homeschooling charter schools which pay for a lot of books, supplies, curricula and museum passes,

In my homeschool community, there are single working moms making it work, single-income families making it work, and even families with two full-time working parents making it work. While some might say they can't afford the time to homeschool, others are doing it.

Committing to being responsible for your children's education is a sacrifice of time and money. But if you feel called to homeschool and know it is what is right for your family, there are very few exceptions which would make it impossible. You may need to make budget changes and sacrifice some extras in life, but if you truly know you're meant to do this, it will be completely worth every sacrifice.

The work you do in educating your children can be considered holy work: fostering deeply-rooted emotional connections, creating a rich family culture that anchors your children's hearts, having the freedom to teach the way your child learns best and thrives, being able to allow the spirit to lead you in the right direction in all of your learning endeavors. I think you'll find there could be no better return on investment than the fruits of this sacred work.

Myth #3:
"I am not _____ enough to homeschool."
(Patient, Smart, Disciplined, Etc.)

I could write pages of adjectives to fill in the blank above about me, and yet here I am writing the book about homeschooling! Do you think any toddler in history who fell on his bottom for the hundredth time while learning to walk thought to himself, "Maybe this walking thing just isn't for me." No! Why do we adults sometimes have such a fixed mindset?

Can you imagine thinking the following about your best friend: "She's not patient enough or smart enough to be a parent." Of course you would never think this! We know that parenting is one of the best ways to refine these attributes.

It's the same with homeschooling. You are qualified to teach your children because you are their parent. No one knows your children better. No one is more emotionally invested or committed to their best interest than you. You are the only one who will walk through fire to help them succeed in life. You are qualified.

But.

If you find you are overwhelmed with too much learning content, find a curriculum that aligns with your beliefs about learning.

> "OUR HOMES ARE THE ULTIMATE SETTING FOR LEARNING, LIVING AND BECOMING."
>
> DAVID A. BEDNAR

If your children need deeper learning than you can provide, learn it with them if it interests you. If it doesn't, find a mentor, join a co-op, find an internship, or find an online course. Technology has created endless opportunities for learning at all levels, pre-school to PhD.

If you're struggling with patience, organization, discipline, or anything else you view as a character flaw, remember that our weaknesses are given to us to keep us humble. With the help of the Lord, we can discover our weaknesses, acknowledge them, learn about them, grow from them, and cultivate them into strengths.

I can't think of a better learning forum for a parent than to spend more time with their own children, who have a way of teaching us about our own weaknesses and strengths. Being a homeschool parent is like a refiner's fire for all character flaws! What better way to become who you want to be than to dive in and learn?

You can teach your children while you're learning. You can serve others while you also need serving. You can help others heal while you're still in your own healing process. Modeling growth and improvement in humans will prove to be one of your child's best character teachers.

Myth #4:
"My child might fall behind state standards."

In so many areas of life, we allow humans to progress at their own speed without questioning their methods or reasons. People attend college at their own pace. They progress in their careers at drastically varying degrees from their peers. If two children of the same age start piano lessons and one masters level 1 faster than the other, no one bats an eye. They chalk it up to different gifts and learning speeds.

If I run a marathon (which I will not), I'll start at the same time as all the other runners but we will all finish at vastly different times. There are so many variables affecting these different times including fitness level, genetics, mindset, and ill-timed nature calls. I, McKenna Gordon, will invariably finish this imaginary race last. But no one would ask me and the fastest runner to pace together—me huffing for air trying to keep up while the fastest runner holds back and waits with me, itching to run ahead.

There isn't a single reason your children should stay at the exact same level as those of their same age. They should be able to move forward to the next level of their education as soon as they are ready, without feeling superior. They should absolutely stay at their current learning level, as long as it is challenging them in healthy ways, without feeling inferior. Society likes to label things as "behind" (bad), "ahead" (cool, but also not good), or "on track" (just right). But there's no developmental research to support these learning standards.

What research shows is that late readers (even extremely late readers) catch up by mid-elementary school, even with little to no intervention. There is also research showing that forcing academics on children too early can result in critical thinking problems, sensory processing issues, and a disdain for reading.

> "CHILDREN ARE NOT A DISTRACTION FROM THE MORE IMPORTANT WORK. THEY ARE THE MOST IMPORTANT WORK."
>
> C.S. LEWIS

National and state-level school standards were not created by educators. They were created by bureaucrats. When Common Core was being developed, they didn't even put one early child expert on the board.

Should we be looking to the school system for how and when children need to learn things? Or is forcing children to uphold these arbitrary milestones when they aren't developmentally ready doing more harm than good?

Myth #5:
"My children won't listen to me as their teacher."

In some aspects, this is true. Because your home is your child's safe place and you are likely your child's safe person, they will feel more comfortable displaying all of their emotions to you. In less safe places, they will tend to stuff emotions in and save them for later. At home, your child will experience outbursts of excitement, curiosity, joy, frustration, annoyance, and self-defeat. The question you need to ask yourself is, "Is this okay with me?" Is it okay with you that your child is able to freely express all of his emotions because you are his safe person?

If it's okay, then ask yourself if your child expressing himself *interferes* with his education, is *neutral* to his education, or *expands* his education? Is it possible that the way you respond to your child can make it any three of these things?

In general, large emotions aren't typically expressed in a public school setting—not because they respect their teacher more than they respect you, but because they fear being shamed, embarrassed, or teased to the point of bullying by their peers. Children in a typical school setting will often hide their confusion concerning the topic being taught. They go through the motions with the class even though they don't really understand.

At home, they won't fake it and go through the motions. They'll display their emotions instead. This is a great opportunity! Confronting

> "ONCE UPON A TIME, ALL CHILDREN WERE HOMESCHOOLED. THEY WERE NOT SENT AWAY FROM HOME EACH DAY TO A PLACE JUST FOR CHILDREN, BUT LIVED, LEARNED, WORKED, AND PLAYED IN THE REAL WORLD; ALONGSIDE ADULTS AND OTHER CHILDREN OF ALL AGES."
>
> RACHEL GATHERCOLE

and exploring these emotions and situations in a safe environment shows that you have their best interest at heart, and that you are there to help. As their trust builds over time, they will listen more carefully and express their thoughts and feelings to you in a more appropriate manner. Not because they're required to listen and speak respectfully, but because they view you as being on their team.

Also consider that you may not need your children to listen to you in the same way they listen to a school teacher. They won't need to sit at a desk for seven hours a day listening to lectures or receiving direct instruction. They won't need to line up or go to their stations at certain times. When they're allowed to be at least somewhat self-directed, they become more proactive and begin to take ownership of their education.

As long as you go through a proper deschooling period, homeschooling will give you and your child the opportunity to learn to listen to *each other* because you value what the other has to contribute.

Myth #6:
"Homeschooled children are sheltered from the real world."

This one requires some more self-reflection. Can you define what it means to you to be sheltered from the real world? I hear two prevailing definitions in this myth:

1. Sheltered from challenging social interactions and worldly vices they would come in contact with in public schools

2. Sheltered from the world that we as adults live and work in?

Homeschooled children may be somewhat sheltered from the first one, but not the second. They generally have more opportunities to engage in the "real world" that we as adults live in. Instead of being surrounded only by children their own age all day long, homeschoolers in general get to experience lots of time with people of all ages: younger children, older children, adults, the elderly. Because of this, they are more confident in interacting with and understanding all ages. Go to any homeschool meet-up or playgroup, and you will find children of all ages playing and working together. No one is deemed too old or too young to play.

I once heard an analogy about homeschool being like a greenhouse. The purpose of a greenhouse is to provide the ideal environment for seedlings to grow and to develop strong roots. It shelters from harmful elements while allowing abundant exposure to what feeds it best: light. As it nears maturity, the gardener puts the plant outside a little at a time until it is able to withstand the full range of outside exposure.

The home is the ideal environment for raising children. A child learns to be an adult by being around adults. As they grow, they will get to experience the outside world a little at a time—under the watchful eye of the parent. One day they will leave the greenhouse with strong roots, ready to flourish and produce good fruit that will benefit the world.

There is no other place in "the real world" that looks like school. Sitting at a desk most of the day, doing as you're told when you're told in concert with a large group, raising your hand to speak or to use the bathroom, with only a few minutes of designated times to be able to talk to and socialize with friends—this just does not occur anywhere in the real world except schooling or prison.

Let's turn this question around: what are public schooled children being sheltered from?

Myth #7:
"My children will fight all the time if I homeschool."

Look, I'm never going to tell you that my children don't bicker. They do. But the story I hear over and over about children fighting as homeschoolers goes something like this: "When my children were in school, they would come home in the afternoon and fight incessantly. But as soon as I pulled them out of school, they began spending more time with each other and fought a lot less."

Why? What causes this miraculous phenomenon?

Is it possible that they rarely see each other when everyone is in public school, so there's little quality time to bond except after school when they're exhausted and the weekends? No healthy relationship ever got better or stronger by avoidance or absence. What is more likely to happen is your children will grow closer together if they are schooled together.

Is it possible that the bickering, picking, and fighting between siblings is modeled behavior from what is happening at school? You decide. A period of deschooling spent in fostering family connections and fun will bring siblings together as best friends and teammates. They'll still quarrel at times, probably even daily in short spurts, but for the most part, they'll hold appreciation and camaraderie for each other.

Myth #8:
"Homeschooled children miss out on important experiences."

Are we talking about prom here? Because there *is* homeschool prom, and it looks nothing like that meme you've seen floating around where the teenager in a dental halo is dancing with his mom in his balloon-laden basement. Homeschool proms in my area put my public high school prom to shame. So bougie!

Oh, this isn't about prom?

Fine. Yes, homeschooled children might miss out on certain experiences that can only happen in a public school setting. But if you're willing to look at it from another angle, children attending public school miss out on some great experiences, too.

Sometimes we adults look back at our childhood and, as we inventory our favorite memories and experiences, we decide we must recreate our favorite experiences in our childrens' lives. This is good and noble—but it's not necessary. What we need to create are the feelings of love, joy, creativity, and adventure those memories bring back, not the exact experience itself.

For example, a friend felt that homeschooling robs children of certain rites of passage—like having a horrible high school teacher that you just couldn't get along with and the lessons and grit that provides to a teenager. Valid. But is having a horrible teacher the *only* way to experience that particular flavor of growth? Could another experience possibly provide that exact same growth?

Between field trip groups, nature groups, dance clubs, sports clubs, service projects, mentorships, internships, tons more family time, more time for exploring passions or mastering an instrument or art form, we have never felt like our children are missing out on any positive experience. And I'm completely fine with them having missed out on any negative experiences that don't contribute to one's growth and development.

Myth #9:
"I will get sick of my children."

Generally when people worry about this, what they're actually fearful of is never getting any alone time. We all need alone time, downtime, zone-out time, and personal time to work on projects without interruption.

Just like your children will learn to bicker less, listen to you more, and realize you're on their team, they will also come to respect time that you set aside for yourself, especially as they get older.

Having no alone time is a bigger concern while children are young. They need a lot of time and care and attention. Small children are a whole lot of work! It's normal and okay to feel overwhelmed and to ask for help or a break. Institute a daily quiet time where everyone takes a break from each other. Train older siblings how to safely watch younger siblings while you get quiet time in your room or work on a project or your business.

As your children get older, you'll find your need to have a break from them lessens greatly. My young teenager is one of my best friends. He's hilarious and intelligent and I love it when he's around. My 10 year old and my 7 year old are now old enough that when I ask for a time out, they'll give it to me—and sometimes they'll do sweet things to make sure my break is a nice one. I'll hear them in the hall whispering, "We should be a little quieter so Mom can concentrate. Maybe it would be nice if we surprised her with clean bedrooms, too." (For the record, that has never actually happened, but I swear I heard it whispered once. Good intentions.)

I came across a meme that made me laugh recently. It said to tell your children, "Hey, I'm going to take a nap. Wake me up in 30 minutes and then we'll clean the house. You'll get the best nap ever." When you're at your wits end, there's always reverse-psychology.

Myth #10: "High school subjects are difficult to teach at home."

With so many resources for homeschoolers, junior high and high school level learning has been so much easier for me than elementary grades. There are online classes, tutoring options, online concurrent enrollment with colleges, internships in a specific area of interest, curriculum written specifically for high schoolers to work through independently, scholar classes through a commonwealth school, and they can still participate in and help teach the family-school learning subjects.

You do not need to be able to teach every high school subject. As your children get older, your role can slowly morph from teacher to facilitator and mentor. Follow their interests and help hook them up with cool opportunities to immerse themselves in what they love.

Once your child nears high school age, you can start making the decision on whether you'll be diploma-seeking or not. A good majority of U.S. colleges have specific enrollment criteria for homeschool students. Colleges love admitting homeschool students because they largely succeed in their programs, which makes the colleges look good. In many cases, what they're looking for is: 1) Good ACT scores; and 2) Excellent character, demonstrated through a history of service opportunities and explained in a good entry essay. At the time of this writing, they don't care about a diploma or a GED, so unless you're in a state that requires one, I personally wouldn't worry about it. Your child may have an opportunity, through internships and other experiences, to enter the workforce directly or to choose a trade school rather than a traditional four-year college. Become familiar with these options. As your child grows and their mission and passions become clear, you can mentor them through developing an appropriate plan for their future.

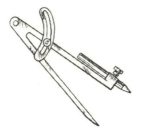

12. Your Custom Blueprint

Anyone who feels the call to homeschool can find a way to do it. When you realize that it can be something that you create and build *around* your living (around your sleep rhythm, family meals, traditions and togetherness, resting, hobbies) rather than the other way around, it can be a source of fulfillment and joy rather than a task.

There will be seasons wherein it begins to feel like a task. Use that feeling as an alarm clock: it's time to mix things up, take a break, slow down, and breathe in a little more *life*. This is not only okay, but necessary for a well-balanced education.

I'd like to continue the story of my son, who inspired us to start homeschooling. I'm not going to tell you that it saved his brain overnight. Because of his giftedness, it is incredibly difficult to challenge his thinking brain, yet very easy to challenge his executive function and to trigger his perfectionism. But over time, deschooling his brain away from those "kill-and-drill" worksheets and the need to perform, measure up, and behave *healed him*. He still does perform, measure up, and behave, but the *reason* he does these things has changed. He improves himself because he wants to and because he recognizes the growth within himself when he does.

Through homeschool, he is allowed to advance several grades of math in three months when his brain is ready for a growth spurt and he's craving it. He's also allowed to go very slow in math during periods of time when he's diving deep into a study of Shakespeare or getting ready to certify as a drone pilot. He has learned to take the driver's seat in his education, with his parents as his mentors. As his mentors, we sometimes need to push him and be the warrior football coach. Sometimes we need to play the role of a soft healer-mentor. Sometimes we recognize that the best way to mentor him is to get out of his way and let him fly! As our other children get older, we're able to support them in these same ways, but unique to their needs.

Since our extra-curricular activities can take place in the middle of the day, our afternoons and evenings are free, affording us so much more family time than we had before homeschooling, and more friend and social time, as well.

> "IT IS A TIME TO DO WHAT IS RIGHT, REGARDLESS OF THE CONSEQUENCES THAT MIGHT FOLLOW. WE HAVE NOTHING TO FEAR. GOD IS AT THE HELM."
>
> THOMAS S. MONSON

One of the surprise perks of homeschooling is how much it has blessed *me* and not just my children. I have greatly broadened and deepened my own education. One concern many parents have about homeschooling is that they will have to learn more things in order to teach them to their children. But when you stop associating learning with discomfort, it doesn't feel like learning did back when you were in school. It doesn't feel like a chore, because there's no test or grade or fear attached. Just simple and free exploration of ideas, connections, and insights on how the world operates. It's fun! I'm a lifelong scholar because of the joy I get from always learning and growing.

You were the first educator of your child. Now, you can become the most effective educator for your child, if you want to. If you feel called to it. Your homeschool can be whatever you make it! It can be around your kitchen table. It can be cuddled up on a huge bed. It can be in the mountains discovering nature together. It can be poring through curriculum that you bought, or it can be free-forming it with library finds, documentaries, internships, and board games. You can spend tons of money or you can do it completely free. The resources are endless and the world is your oyster.

> "Any child who can spend an hour or two a day, or more if he wants, with adults that he likes, who are interested in the world and like to talk about it, will on most days learn far more from their talk than he would learn in a week of school."
>
> John Holt

As you look back through the journaling pages of this book, you will find a custom blueprint for success in beginning your homeschool journey. If you truly looked inward to discover your own beliefs, gifts, and family needs, this blueprint will be the perfect place to start. More perfect than what any veteran homeschooler, professional educator, supermom life-coach, or mother-in-law could dictate or design for you. This is your family's blueprint for maximizing learning and minimizing stress.

Of course, things will change over time as seasons of life ebb and flow, and as your children age. Consider your blueprint as a living document that flows with the needs of your family.

Come back to it each year to make adjustments and reflect on what you learned and how your views have changed.

Come back to it when burnout feels imminent, as you'll find it will likely have the answer on how to rest and recharge. Come back to it when you're tempted to believe that voice in your head telling you that you're not doing enough or that your child won't measure up to state standards. Your blueprint will serve as a mega dose of perspective and truth.

I hope that something I've said here has helped you discover ideas within yourself, inspired a budding excitement for a new way of learning and becoming, quelled worries and doubts, and created a custom education journey upon which you feel joy and confidence in embarking.

Recommended Books, Videos and Resources:

I have read a lot of parenting books. I can't count how many books I've read on educational philosophy. If I've listed it below, it's because it's among the best of the best in my opinion. I cannot recommend the following resources enough.

BOOKS:

Teaching From Rest, Sarah Mackenzie
This is my favorite homeschooling book. I even recommend it to my friends who don't homeschool. If you only read one book from my recommedations, read this one—*especially* if you have concerns about not having enough time or energy to homeschool. It will bring you so much peace and clarity.

The Read-Aloud Family, Sarah Mackenzie
Another one of Sarah's books that I recommend to all parents, whether they homeschool or not. This book has impacted the culture of our family in awesome ways and I think you're going to be very inspired when you read it.

Hold On to Your Kids, Gordon Neufeld
This book is such an eye-opener about the relationships and attachments children make as they grow. This video of Neufeld speaking is almost like an abridged version of the book if you don't want to read the whole thing: https://youtu.be/UlMkWJY5T_w

Christlike Parenting, Glenn Latham
This is such a beautiful parenting book. If you feel you need to work on being a more patient or loving parent, or that you need help enjoying parenthood, this is an excellent book.

Simplicity Parenting, Kim Jon Payne
Another wonderful parenting book that will finally give you the courage and permission to slow down and simplify your family life so there is room for all the things our hearts crave in a family.

The Vanishing American Adult, Ben Sasse
This isn't a homeschooling book at all, but it will probably convince even the most skeptical husband, mother-in-law, or public school educator that homeschooling is a viable option. The way society is raising children now is causing them to be incapable of independently thinking, playing, learning, and working. I know that sounds a little bit gloomy, but it's also very motivating!

Dumbing Us Down, John Taylor Gatto
If you need convincing that the public school system is broken

and does not benefit your child, this is the book. Written by an award-winning public school teacher.

VIDEOS:

Don't miss any of these videos! Watch them with your spouse or listen to them like you would a podcast. They are so good!

Hackschooling Makes Me Happy, Logan LaPlante:
https://youtu.be/h11u3vtcpaY

Kids Need Us More Than Friends, Gordon Neufeld:
https://youtu.be/UlMkWJY5T_w

Simple Joy Conference Keynote, Marlene Peterson:
https://www.youtube.com/watch?v=utLvZQbhOeI

TEDx The Decline of Play, Peter Gray:
https://www.youtube.com/watch?v=Bg-GEzM7iTk

Well Educated Heart Introductory Course:
https://www.welleducatedheart.com/introductory-course.html

Talks from the perspective of
The Church of Jesus Christ of Latter Day Saints

Mothers Who Know, Julie B Beck
https://tinyurl.com/yavueskr

Mothers Teaching Children in the Home, L Tom Perry
https://tinyurl.com/y8ptrm89

Humbly Combining Heart and Mind, LeGrand R. Curtis Jr.
https://tinyurl.com/ydgko73d

Where is Wisdom, Russell M Nelson
https://tinyurl.com/y8wndumw

Learning by Heart, Susan W. Tanner
https://tinyurl.com/yco8dgxn

Seek Learning By Faith, David A. Bednar
https://tinyurl.com/y7h9mw2

Podcasts

The Well-Educated Heart with Marlene Peterson

Moms of Light with Paige Anderson

The Duet Podcast

Child's Name: _____

Subject	Method (Curriculum/Class/ Internship/Other)	Logistics (Family School/Indepen- dent/One-on-one/Other)	Frequency (Daily/Weekly/ Added to loop/Other)

Child's Name: _____

Subject	Method (Curriculum/Class/ Internship/Other)	Logistics (Family School/Independent/One-on-one/Other)	Frequency (Daily/Weekly/ Added to loop/Other)

Child's Name: _____

Subject	Method (Curriculum/Class/Internship/Other)	Logistics (Family School/Independent/One-on-one/Other)	Frequency (Daily/Weekly/Added to loop/Other)

Child's Name: _____

Subject	Method (Curriculum/Class/Internship/Other)	Logistics (Family School/Independent/One-on-one/Other)	Frequency (Daily/Weekly/Added to loop/Other)

Child's Name: _____

Subject	Method (Curriculum/Class/ Internship/Other)	Logistics (Family School/Independent/One-on-one/Other)	Frequency (Daily/Weekly/ Added to loop/Other)

Child's Name: _____

Subject	Method (Curriculum/Class/ Internship/Other)	Logistics (Family School/Independent/One-on-one/Other)	Frequency (Daily/Weekly/ Added to loop/Other)

Child's Name: _____

Subject	Method (Curriculum/Class/ Internship/Other)	Logistics (Family School/Independent/One-on-one/Other)	Frequency (Daily/Weekly/ Added to loop/Other)

Child's Name: _____

Subject	Method *(Curriculum/Class/ Internship/Other)*	Logistics *(Family School/Independent/One-on-one/Other)*	Frequency *(Daily/Weekly/ Added to loop/Other)*

Child's Name: _____

Subject	Method (Curriculum/Class/Internship/Other)	Logistics (Family School/Independent/One-on-one/Other)	Frequency (Daily/Weekly/Added to loop/Other)

About the Author

McKenna Gordon has homeschooled her children since her oldest child was in the first grade. She is a teacher at heart with a gift for distilling the simplicity out of complicated things in life. As a lifelong scholar of all things that fascinate her, McKenna has become a holistic nutritionist, aromatherapist, gardener, painter, and professional musician. She is constantly aware that she will never find enough time to dedicate to all of her learning passions. McKenna encourages many through her blog and website, www.happyathomeschool.com, as well as through her online courses and speaking engagements. Her goal is to help strenghten the homeschooling parent and create deeper connections at home.

Get the audiobook and companion journal at
www.happyathomeschool.com

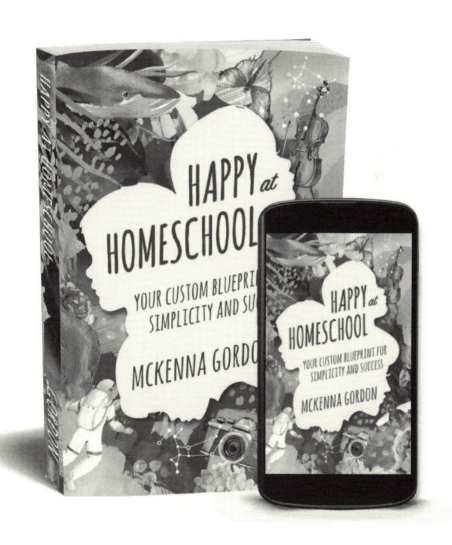

Made in the USA
Middletown, DE
12 July 2021

44042263R00104